French Symbolist Poetry

French
Symbolist
Poetry

TRANSLATED BY C. F. MacINTYRE

ɛley, Los Angeles, London

IVERSITY OF CALIFORNIA PRESS

A LA MÉMOIRE DE
YVES-GÉRARD LE DANTEC
HOMME DE LETTRES, POÈTE, AMI

University of California Press
Berkeley and Los Angeles, California
University of California Press, Ltd.
London, England
© 1958, 2007 by
The Regents of the University of California

ISBN: 978-0-520-25420-6 (pbk. : alk.)

Library of Congress Catalog Card No. 58-10289
Designed by John B. Goetz
Printed in the United States of America

14   13   12   11
08   07   06   05   04

The paper used in this publication meets the minimum
requirements of ANSI/NISO Z39.48-1992 (R 1997)
(*Permanence of Paper*). ∞

PREFACE

Something exciting is always going on in France. An empire has been established, or overthrown. A cabinet has been ousted, or a pistol shot has closed a career and opened a scandal to the public view. Maybe a score of wild-eyed young men are overturning busses to make a barricade. Or a group of noisy enthusiasts on the Left Bank is founding a school of poetry and publishing—for two or three months—a little review. Perhaps a thousand art students, dressed like Indians or South Sea Islanders, i.e., in as few clothes as possible, are dancing, drinking, and judging the naked models for the yearly crown. Or some discontented, lank-haired boy, hardly beginning to shave, is taking apart Debussy's disintegrations in a new way, off into realms of pure cacophony. Another may be pasting bits of broken mirrors and apple peelings around a cork or an old chicken bone, alleging stoutly that he is "painting." The bread is being adulterated, the Algerian boys are running a black market on the franc smack in front of the Opera House, or another girl has thrown herself into the Seine. Something exciting is always going on in France—and that means Paris and nowhere else.

The explosion of Symbolism, in the mid-1880's, was a typical excitement. Manifestoes were issued, poets called each other "imbécile," editors of reviews took sides with much heat. Two clever jokesters, Gabriel Vicaire and Henri Beauclair, even invented a poet and published his works, the *Déliquescences d'Adoré Floupette*, a book that was reviewed solemnly and minutely in *Le Temps*, after which the genuine new poets turned the gibe to their own advantage. Later, when the battle was over and the dust had blown away, it became clear that the new men had won. They had revolutionized French poetry. Rhetorical flourishes, factual descriptions, neat statements of moral dicta, were banished; rules of prosody were fractured, vocabulary opened to all comers, syntax squeezed like an accordion. Music was brought in for its own sake, to achieve effects that could not be had from logical arrangements of words. What the poet wished to say, he expressed in terms of something else. As Larousse sums it up:

Le symbolisme fut une réaction contre l'art des Parnassiens, art tout représentatif, qui consiste soit dans la reproduction des formes et des couleurs, soit dans la transcription logique des idées. Telle que la conçurent les nouveaux poètes, la poésie devait traduire ce que l'âme recèle de plus profond et presque d'inconscient. Le symbole est fondé sur une correspondance entre deux objets dont l'un, généralement, appartient au monde physique, l'autre au monde moral. D'ailleurs, le symbolisme ne consiste pas à faire des symboles en forme, suivis et longuement développés. Pour être symboliste, il suffit d'exprimer les secrètes affinités des choses avec notre âme. Si l'école parnassienne se rattachait au réalisme, si son art était une représentation directe, le symbolisme s'y oppose comme étant une sorte d'évocation. . . .

An earlier poetic revolution had overthrown Romanticism. Gautier's "L'Art," which everybody read in his *Émaux et camées,* in 1858, expressed the new doctrine that has endured in classical verse even through the work of Valéry. Despite the laudable efforts of Mr. Santayana, the poem remains untranslatable; but the essence is contained in the first stanza:

> Oui, l'œuvre sort plus belle
> D'une forme au travail
> Rebelle,
> Vers, marbre, onyx, émail,

and is crystallized in the finale:

> Sculpte, lime, ciselle;
> Que ton rêve flottant
> Se scelle
> Dans le bloc résistant.

Here is the cornerstone of the Parnassian edifice. Baudelaire dedicated his book to the Master, Mallarmé wrote him the fine "Toast funèbre," Leconte de Lisle faithfully carried out the theories and passed them to Heredia, whose *Trophées* are perhaps the culmination, though not the end, of the credo's tenets. The cool verses of Samain, the carven sonnets of Régnier, and the earlier sonnets of Valéry are a permanent part of the Parnassian tradition, plus a profound Baudelairean influence.

It is in the work of Baudelaire that we come to a definite fork in the road. His "Bénédiction" is the swan song of the sad rejected poet in this harsh world, ergo, the finale of the Romantic. "L'Homme et la mer," Nature and man in an eternal struggle, puts the quietus to Mother Nature as man's great friend and protector. Finally he rids his work of the Gothic element of horror and the macabre; nevertheless, he has left his disciples the heritage of *décadence*. On the other hand, "La Beauté" with its famous

> Je hais le mouvement qui déplace les lignes,
> Et jamais je ne pleure et jamais je ne ris

and "Avec ses vêtements" (the frigid and sterile woman, composed mostly of steel, pearl, diamonds, gold, and light) are as Parnassian and statuesque as Leconte's tombstone. Romanticism is dead, long live the Parnassians!

But two other impetuses were implicit in Baudelaire's work. The first is that sinister, ironic quality that begat his "left-handed sons," Verlaine, Corbière, Rimbaud, and Laforgue. These have the same "imp of the perverse," the accursed influence of Saturn.

> We are the sons of Negative
> who never will do right,
> but spend our forces sensitive
> against the "sons of light."

And oddly enough, in this war-threatened world, it is these disruptive spirits who offer more consolation than do the calm Classicists, with their nymphs, fountains, and cool mirrored interiors of moth-eaten salons at Versailles.

It is easy to observe the other influence in Mallarmé's elusive preciosity in pure form and in the mathematically constructed tower of Valéry's escape, for here we discover

vii

the little bacillus of Symbolism, something that evades the filters of analysis. Even the critics have muffed it! Yet most of the later important poets have got it. It is prevalent as hay fever in a rag-weed patch. Symbolism's first stage appearance is said to have been in "Harmonie du soir," with its strange mingling of the senses: fragrant flowers, melancholy waltzes, violin quiverings, curdling blood and dizzy languors. But its permanent springboard is that dubious line in "Correspondances,"

> Les parfums, les couleurs et les sons se répondent.

And the first steps of the run may be discerned in Gérard de Nerval's "Vers dorés," the poem with which we begin.

C. F. M.

ACKNOWLEDGMENT

Grateful acknowledgment is hereby made to Librairie Gallimard, Paris, and The Bollingen Foundation, New York, for their kind permission to use the five poems by Paul Valéry which are translated in this book.

CONTENTS

ix

The Poems

Gérard de Nerval

VERS DORÉS

Eh quoi! tout est sensible!
PYTHAGORE

Homme, libre penseur! te crois-tu seul pensant
Dans ce monde où la vie éclate en toute chose?
Des forces que tu tiens ta liberté dispose,
Mais de tous tes conseils l'univers est absent.

Respecte dans la bête un esprit agissant;
Chaque fleur est une âme à la Nature éclose;
Un mystère d'amour dans le métal repose;
"Tout est sensible!" Et tout sur ton être est puissant.

Crains, dans le mur aveugle, un regard qui t'épie:
A la matière même un verbe est attaché...
Ne la fais pas servir à quelque usage impie!

Souvent dans l'être obscur habite un dieu caché;
Et, comme un œil naissant couvert pas ses paupières,
Un pur esprit s'accroît sous l'écorce des pierres!

GOLDEN VERSES

Eh, what! everything is sentient!
PYTHAGORAS

You, free thinker, imagine only man
thinks in this world where life bursts from all things?
The powers within prescribe your freedom's wings,
but you leave the universe outside your plans.

Respect the mind that stirs in every creature:
love's mystery is known by metals too;
every flower opens its soul to Nature;
"Everything's sentient!" and works on you.

Beware! from the blind wall one watches you:
even matter has a logos all its own . . .
do not put it to some impious use.

Often in humble life a god works, hidden;
and like a new-born eye veiled by its lids,
pure spirit grows beneath the surface of stones.

DELFICA

Ultima Cumaei venit jam carminis aetas.

La connais-tu, Dafné, cette ancienne romance,
Au pied du sycomore, ou sous les lauriers blancs,
Sous l'olivier, le myrte, ou les saules tremblants,
Cette chanson d'amour que toujours recommence?...

Reconnais-tu le Temple au péristyle immense,
Et les citrons amers où s'imprimaient tes dents,
Et la grotte fatale aux hôtes imprudents,
Où du dragon vaincu dort l'antique semence?...

Ils reviendront, ces dieux que tu pleures toujours!
Le temps va ramener l'ordre des anciens jours;
La terre a tressailli d'un souffle prophétique...

Cependant la sibylle au visage latin
Est endormie encor sous l'arc de Constantin
—Et rien n'a dérangé le sévère Portique.

DELFICA

Ultima Cumaei venit jam carminis aetas.

Daphne, you know this ancient melody,
under the shining laurels, beneath the plane,
the myrtle, the trembling willows, or olive tree,
this song of love that always begins again? . . .

Remember the Temple with its mighty pillars,
and the bitter citrons you marked with your teeth?
And the grotto fatal to reckless visitors,
where the old brood of the vanquished dragon sleeps? . . .

These gods you weep for will come, soon or late!
Time will restore the order of ancient days;
the shuddering earth has breathed a prophetic sign . . .

meanwhile the sibyl with the Latin face
still sleeps beneath the Arch of Constantine
—and nothing has disturbed that austere Gate.

MYRTHO

Je pense à toi, Myrtho, divine enchanteresse,
Au Pausilippe altier, de mille feux brillant,
A ton front inondé des clartés d'Orient,
Aux raisins noirs mêlés avec l'or de ta tresse.

C'est dans ta coupe aussi que j'avais bu l'ivresse,
Et dans l'éclair furtif de ton œil souriant,
Quand aux pieds d'Iacchus on me voyait priant,
Car la Muse m'a fait l'un des fils de la Grèce.

Je sais pourquoi là-bas le volcan s'est rouvert...
C'est qu'hier tu l'avais touché d'un pied agile,
Et de cendres soudain l'horizon s'est couvert.

Depuis qu'un duc normand brisa tes dieux d'argile,
Toujours, sous les rameaux du laurier de Virgile,
Le pâle hortensia s'unit au myrte vert!

MYRTHO

Myrtho, I think of you, divine enchantress,
of proud Posilipo and its thousand bright
fires, of your forehead bathed with orient light,
and black grapes mingled in your golden tresses.

It is from your cup I drank to drunkenness,
from the furtive lightning of your smiling eyes,
when at the feet of Bacchus they saw me lie,
praying,—the Muse had made me a son of Greece.

I know why the volcano stirs and thunders . . .
your nimble feet touched it but yesterday,
and suddenly the horizon is covered with cinders.

Since a Norman duke hurled down your gods of clay,
always, beneath the laurel branches of Vergil,
the pale hortensia unites with the green myrtle!

FANTAISIE

Il est un air pour qui je donnerais
Tout Rossini, tout Mozart et tout Weber;
Un air très vieux, languissant et funèbre,
Qui pour moi seul a des charmes secrets.

Or, chaque fois que je viens à l'entendre,
De deux cents ans mon âme rajeunit:
C'est sous Louis-Treize... Et je crois voir s'étendre
Un coteau vert que le couchant jaunit;

Puis un château de brique à coins de pierre,
Aux vitraux teints de rougeâtres couleurs,
Ceint de grands parcs, avec une rivière
Baignant ses pieds, qui coule entre des fleurs;

Puis une dame, à sa haute fenêtre,
Blonde aux yeux noirs, en ses habits anciens...
Que, dans une autre existence peut-être,
J'ai déjà vue—et dont je me souviens!

FANTASY

There is a tune for which I would give all
Rossini, all of Weber and Mozart,
an old tune, languid and funereal,
that charms me only with its secret art.

Now every time I happen to hear it sung,
my soul grows younger by two centuries:
it's the reign of Louis Treize . . . and I think I see
a green hill yellowed by the setting sun;

then an old brick château with stone corners,
and the leaded glass of the windows, color of rose,
begirt by great parks, where a river flows,
bathing the stones as it glides among the flowers;

then a lady, at the tall window of her chamber,
a blonde with dark eyes, in an old-time gown . . .
whom I have seen before, perhaps, and known
in another existence—and whom I remember!

Charles Baudelaire

ÉLÉVATION

Au-dessus des étangs, au-dessus des vallées,
Des montagnes, des bois, des nuages, des mers,
Par delà le soleil, par delà les éthers,
Par delà les confins des sphères étoilées,

Mon esprit, tu te meus avec agilité,
Et, comme un bon nageur qui se pâme dans l'onde,
Tu sillonnes gaiement l'immensité profonde
Avec une indicible et mâle volupté.

Envole-toi bien loin de ces miasmes morbides;
Va te purifier dans l'air supérieur,
Et bois, comme une pure et divine liqueur,
Le feu clair qui remplit les espaces limpides.

Derrière les ennuis et les vastes chagrins
Qui chargent de leur poids l'existence brumeuse
Heureux celui qui peut d'une aile vigoureuse
S'élancer vers les champs lumineux et sereins;

Celui dont les pensers, comme des alouettes,
Vers les cieux le matin prennent un libre essor,
—Qui plane sur la vie et comprend sans effort
Le langage des fleurs et des choses muettes!

ELEVATION

Above the valleys and above the meres,
over woods and mountains, clouds and ocean, past
the sun, the depths of ether, and the vast
utmost boundaries of the starry spheres,

my spirit, you are nimble in your flight,
like a good swimmer blissful in the billow;
gaily through the profound void you furrow
with an ineffable and male delight.

Fly far away from these unhealthful vapors,
go purify yourself in loftier air,
drinking, like a pure and heavenly liquor,
the limpid space that brims with shining fire.

Beyond the boredoms, the immense chagrins
which weight our foggy lives with their dark burden,
happy is he who can with vigorous wings
win to the serene and radiant gardens;

happy the man whose thoughts, like blithe larks flying
in the skies of morning, freely use their powers
—who, hovering over life, knows without trying
the tongues of silent things and of the flowers.

CORRESPONDANCES

La Nature est un temple où de vivants piliers
Laissent parfois sortir de confuses paroles;
L'homme y passe à travers des forêts de symboles
Qui l'observent avec des regards familiers.

Comme de longs échos qui de loin se confondent
Dans une ténébreuse et profonde unité,
Vaste comme la nuit et comme la clarté,
Les parfums, les couleurs et les sons se répondent.

Il est de parfums frais comme des chairs d'enfants,
Doux comme les hautbois, verts comme les prairies,
—Et d'autres, corrompus, riches et triomphants,

Ayant l'expansion des choses infinies,
Comme l'ambre, le musc, le benjoin et l'encens,
Qui chantent les transports de l'esprit et des sens.

CORRESPONDENCES

Nature is a temple of living pillars
where often words emerge, confused and dim;
and man goes through this forest, with familiar
eyes of symbols always watching him.

Like prolonged echoes mingling far away
in a unity tenebrous and profound,
vast as the night and as the limpid day,
perfumes, sounds, and colors correspond.

There are perfumes as cool as children's flesh,
sweet as oboes, as meadows green and fresh;
—others, triumphant and corrupt and rich,

with power to fill the infinite expanses,
like amber, incense, musk, and benzoin, which
sing the transports of the soul and senses.

HARMONIE DU SOIR

Voici venir les temps où vibrant sur sa tige
Chaque fleur s'évapore ainsi qu'un encensoir;
Les sons et les parfums tournent dans l'air du soir;
Valse mélancolique et langoureux vertige!

Chaque fleur s'évapore ainsi qu'un encensoir;
Le violon frémit comme un cœur qu'on afflige;
Valse mélancolique et langoureux vertige!
Le ciel est triste et beau comme un grand reposoir.

Le violon frémit comme un cœur qu'on afflige,
Un cœur tendre, qui hait le néant vaste et noir!
Le ciel est triste et beau comme un grand reposoir;
Le soleil s'est noyé dans son sang qui se fige.

Un cœur tendre, qui hait le néant vaste et noir,
Du passé lumineux recueille tout vestige!
Le soleil s'est noyé dans son sang qui se fige...
Ton souvenir en moi luit comme un ostensoir!

EVENING HARMONY

This is the time when each vibrating flower,
like a censer, is breathing forth its scent;
perfumes and sounds in the evening air are blent;
melancholy waltz and dizzy languor!

Each flower, like a censer, breathes its scent;
the violin quivers, like a heart that suffers;
melancholy waltz and dizzy languor!
The sky, like an altar, is sad and magnificent.

The violin quivers, like a heart that suffers,
hating the Nothing's vast and black extent!
The sky, like an altar, is sad and magnificent;
drowning in curdled blood, the sun sinks lower.

A heart that hates the Nothing's black extent
each vestige of past radiance must gather!
Drowning in curdled blood, the sun sinks lower; . . .
your memory shines in me like the Sacrament!

SPLEEN

J'ai plus de souvenirs que si j'avais mille ans.

Un gros meuble à tiroirs encombré de bilans,
De vers, de billets doux, de procès, de romances,
Avec de lourds cheveux roulés dans des quittances,
Cache moins de secrets que mon triste cerveau.
C'est une pyramide, un immense caveau,
Qui contient plus de morts que la fosse commune.
—Je suis un cimetière abhorré de la lune,
Où comme des remords se traînent de longs vers
Qui s'acharnent toujours sur mes morts les plus chers.
Je suis un vieux boudoir plein de roses fanées,
Où gît tout un fouillis de modes surannées,
Où les pastels plaintifs et les pâles Boucher,
Seuls, respirent l'odeur d'un flacon débouché.

Rien n'égale en longueur les boiteuses journées,
Quand sous les lourds flocons des neigeuses années
L'ennui, fruit de la morne incuriosité,
Prend les proportions de l'immortalité.
—Désormais tu n'es plus, ô matière vivante!
Qu'un granit entouré d'une vague épouvante,
Assoupi dans le fond d'un Saharah brumeux;
Un vieux sphinx ignoré du monde insoucieux,
Oublié sur la carte, et dont l'humeur farouche
Ne chante qu'aux rayons du soleil qui se couche.

SPLEEN

I have more memories than a thousand years.

A bureau, its drawers well stuffed with souvenirs,
verses, love-letters, novels, old processes,
receipted bills wrapped around heavy tresses,
hides fewer secrets than my mournful brains.
This pyramid, this boundless vault, contains
more corpses than the potter's field can hoard.
—I am a graveyard by the moon abhorred,
where, creeping like remorse, the long worms spread
their train to feast upon my dearest dead;
an old boudoir with many a faded rose,
where lies the rummage of outmoded clothes,
where pale Bouchers, pastels in plaintive style
breathe the perfume from an uncorked phial.

None so long as the limping days and slow,
when, under the heavy flakes of years of snow,
Ennui, the fruit of dismal apathy,
assumes the size of immortality.
—Thereafter, living matter, you lie here
like a granite block surrounded by vague fear,
drowsy in the Sahara's hazy waste;
an old sphinx scanted by a world in haste,
omitted from the maps, whose savage whim
sings only when the sunset falls on him.

OBSESSION

Grands bois, vous m'effrayez comme des cathédrales;
Vous hurlez comme l'orgue; et dans nos cœurs maudits,
Chambres d'éternel deuil où vibrent de vieux râles,
Répondent les échos de vos *De profundis*.

Je te hais, Océan! tes bonds et tes tumultes,
Mon esprit les retrouve en lui; ce rire amer
De l'homme vaincu, plein de sanglots et d'insultes,
Je l'entends dans le rire énorme de la mer.

Comme tu me plairais, ô nuit! sans ces étoiles
Dont la lumière parle un langage connu!
Car je cherche le vide, et le noir, et le nu!

Mais les ténèbres sont elles-mêmes des toiles
Où vivent, jaillissant de mon œil par milliers,
Des êtres disparus aux regards familiers.

OBSESSION

Great woods, you frighten me like the cathedrals;
you howl like organs; in our curs'd hearts lie
chapels of endless grief where old râles rattle,
echoing your De Profundis a reply.

Ocean, I hate your tossing and your tumults,
my spirit finds them all again in me;
I hear in the monstrous laughter of the sea
the bitter laugh of the vanquished, with sobs and insults.

O night, how you would please me without stars
whose light speaks only in the banal tongue!
I seek the black, the empty, and the bare!

But the shadows are themselves a canvas where
from my eyes a thousand ghosts are flung,
of vanished beings with familiar stares.

LE SOLEIL

Le long du vieux faubourg, où pendent aux masures
Les persiennes, abri des secrètes luxures,
Quand le soleil cruel frappe à traits redoublés
Sur la ville et les champs, sur les toits et les blés,
Je vais m'exercer seul à ma fantasque escrime,
Flairant dans tous les coins les hasards de la rime,
Trébuchant sur les mots comme sur les pavés,
Heurtant parfois des vers depuis longtemps rêvés.

Ce père nourricier, ennemi des chloroses,
Éveille dans les champs les vers comme les roses;
Il fait s'évaporer les soucis vers le ciel,
Et remplit les cerveaux et les ruches de miel.
C'est lui qui rajeunit les porteurs de béquilles
Et les rend gais et doux comme des jeunes filles,
Et commande aux moissons de croître et de mûrir
Dans le cœur immortel qui toujours veut fleurir!

Quand, ainsi qu'un poète, il descend dans les villes,
Il ennoblit le sort des choses les plus viles,
Et s'introduit en roi, sans bruit et sans valets,
Dans tous les hôpitaux et dans tous les palais.

THE SUN

Along the old slums where the ruined shutters
hang, where secret vices find a shelter,
when the harsh sun's darts with redoubled heat
fall on town and field, on the roofs and the wheat,
I practice my fantastic fencing alone,
stumbling on words as if on paving stones,
sniffing in every corner for chance rhymes,
colliding with verses dreamed at other times.

This foster-father, enemy of chlorosis,
wakens in the fields both poems and roses;
he turns to vapor the troubles of our lives,
and fills with honey the brains and the beehives.
It is he restores the cripples, bids them be
gay and fresh as young girls; it is he
commands the harvest to multiply and mature
in the deathless heart which would always be in flower

Shining on the cities, he exalts,
like a poet, all he sees, despite its faults,
and enters like a king, without noise or vassals,
all the hospitals and all the castles.

Paul Verlaine

APRÈS TROIS ANS

Ayant poussé la porte étroite qui chancelle,
Je me suis promené dans le petit jardin
Qu'éclairait doucement le soleil du matin,
Pailletant chaque fleur d'une humide étincelle.

Rien n'a changé. J'ai tout revu: l'humble tonnelle
De vigne folle avec les chaises de rotin...
Le jet d'eau fait toujours son murmure argentin
Et le vieux tremble sa plainte sempiternelle.

Les roses comme avant palpitent; comme avant,
Les grands lys orgueilleux se balancent au vent.
Chaque alouette qui va et vient m'est connue.

Même j'ai retrouvé debout la Velléda,
Dont le plâtre s'écaille au bout de l'avenue.
—Grêle, parmi l'odeur fade du réséda.

AFTER THREE YEARS

Pushing the narrow sagging gate aside,
I walked into the little garden-bower
which the sun, that morning, softly glorified,
bespangling with wet sparks the smallest flower.

Nothing had changed. I saw it all: the humble
trellis of wild vine, the rattan chairs . . .
the fountain murmuring its silver air,
the old aspen everlastingly atremble.

Just as they used to be: the quivering rose,
the haughty lily on the wind-swayed stalk.
I still know every lark that comes and goes.

I found the Veleda standing even yet,
her plaster scaling, at the end of the walk
—gracile, in the dull scent of mignonette.

CROQUIS PARISIEN

La lune plaquait ses teintes de zinc
      Par angles obtus.
Des bouts de fumée en forme de cinq
Sortaient drus et noirs des hauts toits pointus.

Le ciel était gris, la bise pleurait
      Ainsi qu'un basson.
Au loin, un matou frileux et discret
Miaulait d'étrange et grêle façon.

Moi, j'allais, rêvant du divin Platon
      Et de Phidias,
Et de Salamine et de Marathon,
Sous l'œil clignotant des bleus becs de gaz.

PARISIAN SKETCH

The moon was laying her plates of zinc
      on the oblique.
Like figure fives the plumes of smoke
rose thick and black from the tall roof-peaks.

In the gray sky the breeze wept loud
      as a bassoon.
In a funk a stealthy tomcat miaowed,
far away, his shrill strange tune.

Dreaming of Plato, I walked on,
      and of Phidias,
of Salamis and Marathon,
under winking eyes of blue jets of gas.

CHANSON D'AUTOMNE

Les sanglots longs
Des violons
   De l'automne
Blessent mon cœur
D'une langueur
   Monotone.

Tout suffocant
Et blême, quand
   Sonne l'heure,
Je me souviens
Des jours anciens
   Et je pleure;

Et je m'en vais
Au vent mauvais
   Qui m'emporte
Deçà, delà,
Pareil à la
   Feuille morte.

AUTUMN SONG

With long sobs
the violin-throbs
   of autumn wound
my heart with languorous
and monotonous
   sound.

Choking and pale
when I mind the tale
   the hours keep,
my memory strays
down other days
   and I weep;

and I let me go
where ill winds blow,
   now here, now there,
harried and sped
even as a dead
   leaf, anywhere.

CLAIR DE LUNE

Votre âme est un paysage choisi
Que vont charmants masques et bergamasques,
Jouant du luth et dansant et quasi
Tristes sous leurs déguisements fantasques.

Tout en chantant sur le mode mineur
L'amour vainqueur et la vie opportune,
Ils n'ont pas l'air de croire à leur bonheur
Et leur chanson se mêle au clair de lune,

Au calme clair de lune triste et beau,
Qui fait rêver les oiseaux dans les arbres
Et sangloter d'extase les jets d'eau,
Les grands jets d'eau sveltes parmi les marbres.

MOONLIGHT

Your soul is like a painter's landscape where
charming masks in shepherd mummeries
are playing lutes and dancing with an air
of being sad in their fantastic guise.

Even while they sing, all in a minor key,
of love triumphant and life's careless boon,
they seem in doubt of their felicity,
their song melts in the calm light of the moon,

the lovely melancholy light that sets
the little birds to dreaming in the tree
and among the statues makes the jets
of slender fountains sob with ecstasy.

IL PLEURE DANS MON CŒUR...

Il pleure doucement sur la ville.
ARTHUR RIMBAUD

Il pleure dans mon cœur
Comme il pleut sur la ville,
Quelle est cette langueur
Qui pénètre mon cœur?

O bruit doux de la pluie
Par terre et sur les toits!
Pour un cœur qui s'ennuie,
O le chant de la pluie!

Il pleure sans raison
Dans ce cœur qui s'écœure.
Quoi! nulle trahison?
Ce deuil est sans raison.

C'est bien la pire peine
De ne savoir pourquoi,
Sans amour et sans haine,
Mon cœur a tant de peine!

IT WEEPS IN MY HEART

It rains gently on the town.
ARTHUR RIMBAUD

It weeps in my heart
as it rains on the town.
What languorous hurt
thus pierces my heart?

Oh, sweet sound of rain
on the earth and the roofs!
For a heart dulled with pain,
oh, the song of the rain!

It weeps without reason
in my disheartened heart.
What! there's no treason?
This grief's without reason.

It's far the worst pain
not to know why,
without love or disdain
my heart has such pain.

LANGUEUR

Je suis l'Empire à la fin de la décadence,
Qui regarde passer les grands Barbares blancs
En composant des acrostiches indolents
D'un style d'or où la langueur du soleil danse.

L'âme seulette a mal au cœur d'un ennui dense.
Là-bas on dit qu'il est de longs combats sanglants.
O n'y pouvoir, étant si faible aux vœux si lents,
O n'y vouloir fleurir un peu de cette existence!

O n'y vouloir, ô n'y pouvoir mourir un peu!
Ah! tout est bu! Bathylle, as-tu fini de rire?
Ah, tout est bu, tout est mangé! Plus rien à dire!

Seul, un poème un peu niais qu'on jette au feu,
Seul, un esclave un peu coureur qui vous néglige,
Seul, un ennui d'on ne sait quoi qui vous afflige!

APATHY

I am the Empire in its *décadence*
watching the tall blond Norsemen march, meanwhile
writing indolently, with a golden style,
acrostics where the sunlight's languors dance.

The lonely soul is heartsick with this dreary
boredom. They say, down there a battle rages.
Ah, if only I weren't so slack and weary,
if I could bloom a bit in this dull age!

If I but had the power and the will
to die a little! Are you laughing still,
Bathyllus? All's been drunk, all eaten—spent!

Only a stupid poem for the fire,
only a pampered slave grown negligent!
Blasé, and not to know what you desire!

ART POÉTIQUE

De la musique avant toute chose,
Et pour cela préfère l'Impair
Plus vague et plus soluble dans l'air,
Sans rien en lui qui pèse ou qui pose.

Il faut aussi que tu n'ailles point
Choisir tes mots sans quelque méprise:
Rien de plus cher que la chanson grise
Où l'Indécis au Précis se joint.

C'est des beaux yeux derrière les voiles,
C'est le grand jour tremblant de midi,
C'est, par un ciel d'automne attiédi,
Le bleu fouillis des claires étoiles!

Car nous voulons la Nuance encor,
Pas la Couleur, rien que la nuance!
Oh, la nuance seule fiance
Le rêve au rêve et la flûte au cor!

Fuis du plus loin la Pointe assassine,
L'Esprit cruel et le rire impur,
Qui font pleurer les yeux de l'Azur,
Et tout cet ail de basse cuisine!

THE ART OF POETRY

You must have music first of all,
and for that a rhythm uneven is best,
vague in the air and soluble,
with nothing heavy and nothing at rest.

You must not scorn to do some wrong
in choosing the words to fill your lines:
nothing more dear than the tipsy song
where the Undefined and Exact combine.

It is the veiled and lovely eye,
the full noon quivering with light;
it is, in the cool of an autumn sky,
the blue confusion of stars at night!

Never the Color, always the Shade,
always the nuance is supreme!
Only by shade is the trothal made
between flute and horn, of dream with dream!

Epigram's an assassin! Keep
away from him, fierce Wit, and vicious
laughter that makes the Azure weep,
and from all that garlic of vulgar dishes!

Prends l'éloquence et tords-lui son cou!
Tu feras bien, en train d'énergie,
De rendre un peu la Rime assagie.
Si l'on n'y veille, elle ira jusqu'où?

O qui dira les torts de la Rime!
Quel enfant sourd ou quel nègre fou
Nous a forgé ce bijou d'un sou
Qui sonne creux et faux sous la lime?

De la musique encore et toujours!
Que ton vers soit la chose envolée
Qu'on sent qui fuit d'une âme en allée
Ver d'autres cieux è d'autres amours.

Que ton vers soit la bonne aventure
Éparse au vent crispé du matin
Qui va fleurant la menthe et le thym...
Et tout le reste est littérature.

Take Eloquence and wring his neck!
You would do well, by force and care,
wisely to hold Rhyme in check,
or she's off—if you don't watch—God knows where!

Oh, who will tell the wrongs of Rhyme?
What crazy negro or deaf child
made this trinket for a dime,
sounding hollow and false when filed?

Let there be music, again and forever!
Let your verse be a quick-wing'd thing and light—
such as one feels when a new love's fervor
to other skies wings the soul in flight.

Happy-go-lucky, let your lines
disheveled run where the dawn winds lure,
smelling of wild mint, smelling of thyme . . .
and all the rest is literature.

Tristan Corbière

LE POÈTE CONTUMACE

Sur la côte d' ARMOR.—Un ancien vieux couvent,
Les vents se croyaient là dans un moulin-à-vent,
  Et les ânes de la contrée,
Au lierre râpé venaient râper leurs dents
Contre un mur si troué que, pour entrer dedans,
  On n'aurait pu trouver l'entrée.

—Seul—mais toujours debout avec un rare aplomb,
Crénelé comme la mâchoire d'une vieille,
Son toit à coups de poing sur le coin de l'oreille,
Aux corneilles bayant, se tenait le donjon.

Fier toujours d'avoir eu, dans le temps, sa légende...
Ce n'était plus qu'un nid à gens de contrebande,
Vagabonds de nuit, amoureux buissonniers,
Chiens errants, vieux rats, fraudeurs et douaniers.

—Aujourd'hui l'hôte était, de la borgne tourelle,
Un Poète sauvage, avec un plomb dans l'aile;
Et tombé là parmi les antiques hiboux
Qui l'estimaient d'en haut.—Il respectait leurs trous,—
Lui, seul hibou payant, comme son *bail* le porte:
Pour vingt-cinq écus l'an, dont: remettre une porte.—

Pour les gens du pays, il ne les voyait pas:
Seulement, en passant, eux regardaient d'en bas,
  Se montrant du nez sa fenêtre;
Le curé se doutait que c'était un lépreux;
Et le maire disait:—Moi, qu'est-ce que j'y peux,
  C'est plutôt un Anglais... un *Être.*

THE CONTUMACIOUS POET

On ARMORICA's seacoast.—An ancient former convent;
the winds, which thought it a windmill, came and went,
    and the donkeys of the country
wore down their teeth on the worn-out ivy stalks
on a wall so full of holes that one could walk
    right in without hunting the entry.

Alone—but upright with aplomb most rare,
its crenellations like an old woman's jaws,
gaping wide at the moon, the tower rose,
its roof by blows of a fist knocked over one ear.

Of having its old-time legend always proud . . .
it was nothing now but a nest for the contraband-crowd,
nocturnal vagabonds, the loving snugglers
in bushes, stray dogs, old rats, revenuers, and smugglers.

—Today this one-eyed tower had as its guest
an unsociable Poet, his wings weighed down with lead;
among the elderly owls he'd tumbled there,
and they sized him up from above.—He respected their nests,—
he, the one paying owl, as his *lease* read:
For twenty-five écus a year: and replace the door.—

He never saw the neighbor-folk, although
when they went past they'd stare up from below,
    at his window pointing their nose;
the priest surmised that he was a leper, no doubt;
and the mayor said:—Me! what can I do about
    the *creature?* . . . English, I suppose.

Les femmes avaient su—sans doute par les buses—
Qu'il *vivait en concubinage avec des Muses!*...
Un hérétique enfin... Quelque *Parisien*
De Paris, ou d'ailleurs?—Hélas! on n'en sait rien.—
Il était invisible; et, comme *ses Donzelles*
Ne s'affichaient pas trop, on ne parla plus d'elles.

—Lui, c'était simplement un long flâneur, sec, pâle;
Un ermite-amateur, chassé par la rafale...
Il avait trop aimé les beaux pays malsains.
Condamné des huissiers, comme des médecins,
Il avait posé là, soûl et cherchant sa place
Pour mourir seul ou pour vivre par contumace...

  Faisant, d'un à peu près d'artiste,
  Un philosophe d'à peu près,
  Râleur de soleil ou de frais,
  En dehors de l'humaine piste.

Il lui restait encore un hamac, une vielle,
Un barbet qui dormait sous le nom de *Fidèle*;
Non moins fidèle était, triste et doux comme lui,
Un autre compagnon qui s'appelait l'Ennui.

Se mourant en sommeil, il se vivait en rêve,
Son rêve était le flot qui montait sur la grève,
  Le flot qui descendait;
Quelquefois, vaguement, il se prenait attendre...
Attendre quoi... le flot monter—le flot descendre—
  Ou l'Absente... Qui sait?

Le sait-il bien lui-même?... Au vent de sa guérite,
A-t-il donc oublié comme les morts vont vite?
Lui, ce viveur vécu, revenant égaré,
Cherche-t-il son follet, à lui, mal enterré?

The women had learned—no doubt from buzzard-news—
that he *lived in concubinage with the Muse!* . . .
Some *Parisian* from Paris . . . in short, an infidel
from somewhere or other?—Alas, no one could tell.—
He was invisible; *his Wenches, they*
didn't publish their presence, there was no more to say.

—He was merely a skinny loafer, dried-up, pale;
an amateur hermit, blown in by the gale . . .
he had loved too well fine lands where fevers brew.
Condemned by bailiffs, and by doctors too,
he'd perched there, fed up, hunting a place to halt
and die alone, or live on by default . . .

> making almost a philosopher
> of an artist only by half,
> a noon-and-evening grumbler
> aside from the human path.

He still had a hammock and a hurdy-gurdy,
a sleepy spaniel—"Faithful" was his name;
and another pal called "Ennui," just as sturdy
in devotion and as melancholy and tame.

Dying in sleep, in dreams he lived the most,
his dream being the tide that climbed the coast,
> the tide that ebbs and flows;
sometimes, vaguely, he would wait . . . what for? . . .
the tide to come in—the tide to ebb from shore—
> or the Absent One . . . who knows?

Does even he know? . . . Has he forgotten the hurried
flight of the dead on the wind by his sentry-post?
This worn-out playboy, this bewildered ghost,
is he seeking his goblin mate, himself badly buried?

—Certes, Elle n'est pas loin, celle après qui tu brâmes,
O Cerf de Saint-Hubert! Mais ton front est sans flammes.
N'apparais pas, mon vieux, triste et faux déterré...
Fais le mort si tu peux... Car Elle t'a pleuré!

—Est-ce qu'il pouvait, Lui!... n'était-il pas poète...
Immortel comme un autre?... Et dans sa pauvre tête
Déménagée, encore il sentait que les vers
Hexamètres faisaient les cent pas de travers.

—Manque de savoir-vivre extrême—il survivait—
Et—manque de savoir-mourir—il écrivait:

"C'est un être passé de cent lunes, ma Chère,
En ton cœur poétique, à l'état légendaire.
Je rime, donc je vis... ne crains pas, c'est *à blanc,*
—Une coquille d'huître en rupture de banc!—
Oui, j'ai beau me palper; c'est moi! Dernière faute—
En route pour les cieux—car ma niche est si haute!—
Je me suis demandé, prêt à prendre l'essor:
Tête ou pile... —Et voilà—je me demande encor..."

"C'est à toi que je fis mes adieux à la vie,
A toi qui me pleuras, jusqu'à me faire envie
De rester me pleurer avec toi. Maintenant
C'est joué, je ne suis qu'un gâteux revenant,
En os et... (j'allais dire en chair).—La chose est sûre.
C'est bien moi, je suis là,—mais comme une rature."

"Nous étions amateurs de curiosité:
Viens voir *le Bibelot.*—Moi j'en suis dégoûté.—
Dans mes dégoûts surtout, j'ai des goûts élégants;
Tu sais: j'avais lâché la Vie avec des gants;
L'*Autre* n'est pas même à prendre avec des pincettes...
Je cherche au mannequin de nouvelles toilettes."

—Sure, She's not far off, she for whom you bellow,
O Stag of Saint Hubert! But you've no flames on your head.
Don't pop out, sad and wrongly dug up, old fellow . . .
act like a corpse if you can . . . for She mourned you as dead!

—But how could He do that? . . . poet, wasn't he . . .
immortal like another? . . . and in his poor head,
with nobody home, he still felt, crookedly,
hexameters marching with a sentry's tread.

—Not knowing how to live, he kept on living—
and not knowing how to die, he went on writing:

"Here's a person who, these many moons, is part
of the legend, Dear, in your poetic heart.
I rhyme, therefore I am . . . never fear, it's a *blank,*
—an oystershell that's being raked from its bank!—
Sure, I have pinched myself; still I am I!
Last error—heaven-bound—for my niche is that high!—
I've kept asking myself: Are you ready for the flight?
Heads or tails . . . —And look—I am asking it yet . . .

"It was to you that I bade life good-bye,
to you who wept over me till finally I
wanted to stay and weep with you. But now I've lost—
the game's played out—I'm only an idiot ghost
with bones and . . . (I was going to say 'flesh').—Past doubt,
it's me, all right, I'm here,—like a thing rubbed out.

"We were fanciers of curiosity:
come see *the Bibelot.*—That's not for me.—
Especially in my dislikes my taste's above
the average; you know: I chucked Life, wearing gloves;
the *Other* can't even be touched with tongs, God knows . . .
I'm eyeing tailor's dummies for new clothes.

"Reviens m'aider: Tes yeux dans ces yeux-là! Ta lèvre
Sur cette lèvre... Et, là, ne sens-tu pas ma fièvre
—Ma *fièvre de Toi*?... —Sous l'orbe est-il passé
L'arc-en-ciel au charbon par nos nuits laissé?
Et cette étoile?... —Oh! va, ne cherche plus l'étoile
        Que tu voulais voir à mon front;
        Une araignée a fait sa toile,
        Au même endroit—dans le plafond."

"Je suis un étranger.—Cela vaut mieux peut-être...
—Eh bien! non, viens encore un peu me reconnaître;
Comme au bon saint Thomas, je veux te voir la foi,
Je veux te voir toucher la plaie et dire:—Toi!—"

"Viens encor me finir—c'est très gai: De ta chambre,
Tu verras mes moissons—nous sommes en décembre—
Mes grands bois de sapins, les fleurs d'or des genêts,
Mes bruyères d'Armor... —en tas sur les chenets.
Viens te gorger d'air pur.—Ici j'ai de la brise
Si franche!... que le bout de ma toiture en frise.
Le soleil est si doux... —qu'il gèle tout le temps.
Le printemps... —Le printemps, n'est-ce pas tes vingt ans?
On n'attend plus que toi, vois: déjà l'hirondelle
Se pose... en fer rouillé, clouée à ma tourelle.—
Et bientôt nous pourrons cueillir le champignon...
Dans mon escalier que dore... un lumignon.
Dans le mur qui verdoie existe une pervenche
Sèche.— ... Et puis nous irons à l'eau *faire* la planche
—Planches d'épave au sec—comme moi—sur ces plages.
La Mer roucoule sa *Berceuse pour naufrages*;
Barcarolle du soir... pour les canards sauvages."

"En *Paul et Virginie*, et virginaux—veux-tu—
Nous nous mettrons au vert du paradis perdu...
Ou *Robinson avec Vendredi*—c'est facile:
La pluie a déjà fait, de mon royaume, une île."

"Come back and help me: Your eyes in these eyes!
Your lips on these! . . . Don't you feel my fever rise—
my *fever for You?* . . . —Has the rainbow taken flight
down under, left in cinders by our nights?
And that star? . . . —That star you wanted to see on my brow,
    forget it, seek it not;
    there's a spider's web there now
    on the ceiling—in the same spot.

"I'm a stranger.—Well, maybe that's for the best . . .
—You mean that? no, come back, sound me out anew;
like good Saint Thomas, I must see you test
your faith as you touch the wound and then say:—You!—

"Come, finish me off—it's amusing: from your chamber
you'll see my harvests—it's already December—
the golden broom-flowers, my great forests of fir,
and, piled on the andirons, my Armorican briar . . . —
Come, gorge on pure air.—Here, I have a breeze
so fresh! . . . it frizzles the edges of my eaves!
The sun is so pleasant . . . —that it's freezing here.
The spring . . . —the spring, isn't that your twenty years?
You're all that's lacking: see that swallow where it
perches . . . in rusty iron, nailed to the turret.—
And soon we can go to my stairs and pick mushrooms . . .
where a candle-end turns all to a golden gloom.
A dry periwinkle on the moss-green flank
of the wall merely exists.— . . . Then we'll *float* like planks
—ship-planks all dried out—same as me—on these rocks.
The Sea croons her *Lullaby for Shipwrecked Folk;*
an evening barcarolle . . . for the wild ducks.

'Like *Paul and Virginia,* and virginal—it would be nice—
we'll live in the green of the lost paradise . . .
or—it's easy—in *Crusoe and Man Friday* style:
rain has already turned my realm to an isle.

"Si pourtant, près de moi, tu crains la solitude,
Nous avons des amis, sans fard: un braconnier;
Sans compter un caban bleu, qui, par habitude,
Fait toujours les cent pas et contient un douanier...
Plus de clercs d'huissier! J'ai le clair de la lune,
Et des amis pierrots amoureux sans fortune."

—"Et nos nuits!... *Belles nuits pour l'orgie à la tour!*...
Nuits à la Roméo!—Jamais il ne fait jour.—
La Nature au réveil—réveil de déchaînée—
Secouant son drap blanc... éteint ma cheminée.
Voici mes rossignols... rossignols d'ouragans—
Gais comme des pinsons—sanglots de chats-huants!
Ma girouette dérouille en haut sa tyrolienne
Et l'on entend gémir ma porte éolienne,
Comme chez saint Antoine en sa tentation...
Oh viens! joli Suppôt de la séduction!"

—"Hop! les rats du grenier dansent des farandoles!
Les ardoises de toit roulent en castagnoles!
Les Folles du logis...
                    Non, je n'ai plus de Folles!"

... "Comme je revendrais ma dépouille à Satan
S'il me tentait avec un petit Revenant...
—Toi—je te vois partout, mais comme un voyant blême,
Je t'adore... Et c'est pauvre: adorer ce qu'on aime!
Apparais, un poignard dans le cœur!—Ce sera,
Tu sais bien, comme dans *Inès de la Sierra*...
—On frappe... oh! c'est quelqu'un...
                    Hélas! oui, c'est un rat.'

"If you're frightened of solitude, here with just me,
we've friends without veneer—one's a poacher, it's true;
without counting a blue coat which, habitually,
makes its rounds and contains a collector of revenue . . .
no more sheriff's clerks! I have moonlight galore,
and some friendly amorous sparrows, very poor.

"And our nights! . . . *Belles nuits pour l'orgie à la tour!* . . .
Nights *à la* Romeo!—Never the sunrise hour.—
Nature at waking—a waking that bursts forth—
throwing aside its white sheet . . . puts out my hearth.
Hear my nightingales . . . hurricane-nightingales—
gay as finches—the brown owl's sobbing wails!
My weathercock rubs the rust from his Tyrolean
yodels, you hear the groans of my Aeolian
hinges, like Saint Anthony's at his temptation . . .
Oh, come, my lovely Votaress of seduction!

—"Hup! the attic rats dance farandoles!
The roof tiles roll around like castagnoles!
My Crotchets . . .
                    No, I've no more Folderols!

. . . "How I'd sell Satan back my skin at cost
if he should tempt me with one little Ghost . . .
—You—I see you everywhere, pale seer,
whom I adore . . . and it's flat: to adore what's dear!
Come forth, with a poniard in your heart!—now, that
would be like *Inès de la Sierra,* pat . . .
—A knock . . . someone, no doubt . . .
                              Alas, yes, a rat.

—"Je rêvasse... et toujours c'est *Toi*. Sur toute chose,
Comme un esprit follet, ton souvenir se pose;
Ma solitude—*Toi!*—Mes hiboux à l'œil d'or:
—*Toi!* Ma girouette folle: oh *Toi!*... —Que sais-je encor...
—*Toi!* mes volets ouvrant les bras dans la tempête...
Une lointaine voix: c'est Ta chanson!—c'est fête!...
Les rafales fouaillant Ton nom perdu—c'est bête—
C'est bête, mais c'est *Toi!* Mon cœur au grand ouvert

       Comme mes volets en pantenne,
       Bat, tout affolé sous l'haleine
       Des plus bizarres courants d'air."

"Tiens... une ombre portée, un instant, est venue
Dessiner ton profil sur la muraille nue,
Et j'ai tourné la tête... —Espoir ou souvenir—
Ma Sœur Anne, à ta tour, voyez-vous pas venir?...
—Rien!—je vois... je vois, dans la froide chambrette,
Mon lit capitonné de *satin de brouette;*
Et mon chien qui dort dessus—pauvre animal—
... Et je ris... parce que ça me fait un peu mal."

"J'ai pris, pour t'appeler, ma vielle et ma lyre,
Mon cœur fait de l'esprit—le sot—pour se leurrer...
Viens pleurer, si mes vers ont pu te faire rire;
       Viens rire, s'ils t'ont fait pleurer... "

"Ce sera drôle... Viens jouer à la misère.
D'après nature:—*Un cœur avec une chaumière.*—
... Il pleut dans mon foyer, il pleut dans mon cœur feu.
Viens! Ma chandelle est morte et je n'ai plus de feu."

Sa lamps se mourait. Il ouvrit la fenêtre.
Le soleil se levait. Il regarda sa lettre,
Rit et la déchira... Les petits morceaux blancs,
Dans la brume, semblaient un vol de goélands.

(Penmarc'h—jour de Noël.)

—"I daydream . . . always it's *You*. Over everything,
your memory hovers on an elfin wing;
my solitude—*You!*—my gold-eyed owls—*You're* that—
my mad windvane: ah, *You!* . . . —what more do I know?
—*You*: my shutters opening their arms to the blast . . .
a far-off voice: it's Your song!—it's a feast! . . .
the squalls are lashing Your lost name—it's utter
nonsense, but it's *You!* My heart, spread far
       open as my blown shutters,
       beats crazily, under the bizarre
       gusts of the breathing air.

"Look . . . a shadow for an instant falls,
drawing your profile on the naked wall,
and I turn my head . . . —Is it hope, or do I hear—
Ma Sœur Anne, à ta tour, voyez-vous pas venir? . . .
—Nothing!—I see . . . I see, in my cold attic,
my bed with its quilting of *best barnyard satin*;
and my dog asleep on it—poor animal—
. . . and I laugh . . . because it makes me a little ill.

"I have taken my hurdy-gurdy and my lyre, to try
to call you back. My heart—that dumb moon-calf—
deludes himself . . . Come weep, if my verse makes you laugh;
       come laugh, if it makes you cry . . .

'Come, let's play Poor Man . . . it's a humorous part.
Back to Nature.—*Love in a straw-thatched hut.*—
. . . It rains on my hearth, it rains on my dead heart.
Come! My candle's dead and my fire is out."

           ◊   ◊   ◊

His lamp was dying. He opened the window-shutter.
The sun was rising. He looked at his letter,
laughed, and tore it up . . . the little white
pieces in the fog seemed gulls in flight.

                           (Penmarc'h—Christmas.)

RONDEL

Il fait noir, enfant, voleur d'étincelles!
Il n'est plus de nuits, il n'est plus de jours;
Dors... en attendant venir toutes celles
Qui disaient: Jamais! qui disaient: Toujours!

Entends-tu leurs pas? Ils ne sont pas lourds:
Oh, les pieds légers!—l'Amour a des ailes...
Il fait noir, enfant, voleur d'étincelles!

Entends-tu leurs voix?... Les caveaux sont sourds.
Dors: il pèse peu, ton faix d'immortelles:
Ils ne viendront pas, tes amis les ours,
Jeter leur pavé sur tes demoiselles:
Il fait noir, enfant, voleur d'étincelles!

DO, L'ENFANT, DO...

Buona vespre! Dors: Ton bout de cierge,
On l'a posé là, puis on est parti.
Tu n'auras pas peur seul, pauvre petit?...
C'est le chandelier de ton lit d'auberge.

Du fesse-cahier ne crains plus la verge,
Va!.... De t'éveiller point n'est si hardi.
Buona sera! Dors: Ton bout de cierge...

Est mort.—Il n'est plus, ici, de concierge:
Seuls, le vent du nord, le vent du midi
Viendront balancer un fil-de-la-Vierge.
Chut! Pour les pieds-plats, ton sol est maudit.
—*Buona notte!* Dors: Ton bout de cierge...

RONDEL

It's getting dark, child, robber of sparks!
There are no more nights, there are no more days;
sleep . . . and wait those who will remark:
Never! and those who will say: Always!

Do you hear their steps? Not heavy, nay:
oh, the light feet!—Love, winged like the larks . . .
it's getting dark, child, robber of sparks!

You hear their voice? . . . Graves are deaf and dark.
Sleep: they weigh little, your immortelles:
your friends the bears will not come, not they,
to throw paving stones at your demoiselles:
it's getting dark, child, robber of sparks!

BY-O, BABY, BY-O!

Buona vespre! Sleep: your bit of taper,
someone put it here, then someone is gone.
You won't be afraid by yourself, poor little one? . . .
It's the candlestick for your bedside in the tavern.

Fear no more the whip of those scribblers on paper,
go! . . . There's no one dares not let you sleep on.
Buona sera! Sleep: your bit of taper . . .

is dead.—There is no longer any doorkeeper:
the wind of the north, the wind of the south, alone,
will come to set your gossamer thread aquiver.
Hush! for the dolts, your clay is malediction.
—*Buona notte!* Sleep: your bit of taper . . .

MIRLITON

Dors d'amour, méchant ferreur de cigales!
Dans le chiendent qui te couvrira
La cigale aussi pour toi chantera,
Joyeuse, avec ses petites cymbales.

La rosée aura des pleurs matinales;
Et le muguet blanc fait un joli drap...
Dors d'amour, méchant ferreur de cigales!

Pleureuses en troupeaux passeront les rafales...

La Muse camarde ici posera,
Sur ta bouche noire encore elle aura
Ces rimes qui vont aux moelles des pâles...
Dors d'amour, méchant ferreur de cigales.

PETIT MORT POUR RIRE

Va vite, léger peigneur de comètes!
Les herbes au vent seront tes cheveux;
De ton œil béant jailliront les feux
Follets, prisonniers dans les pauvres têtes...

Les fleurs de tombeau qu'on nomme Amourettes
Foisonneront plein ton rire terreux...
Et les myosotis, ces fleurs d'oubliettes...

Ne fais pas le lourd: cercueils de poètes
Pour les croque-morts sont de simples jeux,
Boîtes à violon qui sonnent le creux...
Ils te croiront mort—Les bourgeois sont bêtes—
Va vite, léger peigneur de comètes!

MIRLITON

In love, sly smith of cicadas, sleep!
Among your twitch-grass covering
the cicada for you too will sing,
joyous, to his small cymbals' beat.

The dew with morning tears will weep;
and the *muguets* make a fine winding-sheet . . .
in love, sly smith of cicadas, sleep!

Weeping in flocks the squalls will sweep . . .

Here Death the Snub-nosed Muse will cling,
still to your black lips she'll bring
the rhymes that make pale folks' marrow creep . . .
in love, sly smith of cicadas, sleep!

A LITTLE DEATH TO MAKE ONE LAUGH

Go quickly, nimble comber of comets!
Grass in the wind will be hair on your skull;
elf-fires will flash from your hollow sockets,
fires that are prisoned in dullards' polls . . .

the flowers of the grave called Amourettes
will swell your earthy laughter full . . .
and forget-me-nots, flowers of oubliettes . . .

Don't make it heavy: coffins for poets
are easy for hired mutes to follow,
fiddle-boxes that sound hollow . . .
they'll think you are dead—the bourgeois are fools—
go quickly, nimble comber of comets!

Stéphane Mallarmé

SALUT

Rien, cette écume, vierge vers
A ne désigner que la coupe;
Telle loin se noie une troupe
De sirènes mainte à l'envers.

Nous naviguons, ô mes divers
Amis, moi déjà sur la poupe
Vous l'avant fastueux qui coupe
Le flot de foudres et d'hivers;

Une ivresse belle m'engage
Sans craindre même son tangage
De porter debout ce salut

Solitude, récif, étoile
A n'importe ce qui valut
Le blanc souci de notre toile.

A TOAST

Nothing, this foam, virgin verse
denoting only the cup;
thus far away drowns a troop
of sirens many reversed.

We sail, O my diverse
friends, I by now on the poop
you the dashing prow that sunders
the surge of winters and thunders;

a lovely glow prevails
in me without fear of the pitch
to offer upright this toast

Solitude, star, rock-coast
to that no matter which
worth the white concern of our sail

L'APRÈS-MIDI D'UN FAUNE

Églogue

LE FAUNE

Ces nymphes, je les veux perpétuer.

                        Si clair,
Leur incarnat léger, qu'il voltige dans l'air
Assoupi de sommeils touffus.

                    Aimai-je un rêve?
Mon doute, amas de nuit ancienne, s'achève
En maint rameau subtil, qui, demeuré les vrais
Bois mêmes, prouve, hélas! que bien seul je m'offrais
Pour triomphe la faute idéale de roses.
Réfléchissons...

             ou si les femmes dont tu gloses
Figurent un souhait de tes sens fabuleux!
Faune, l'illusion s'échappe des yeux bleus
Et froids, comme une source en pleurs, de la plus chaste:
Mais, l'autre tout soupirs, dis-tu qu'elle contraste
Comme brise du jour chaude dans ta toison?
Que non! par l'immobile et lasse pâmoison
Suffoquant de chaleurs le matin frais s'il lutte,
Ne murmure point d'eau que ne verse ma flûte
Au bosquet arrosé d'accords; et le seul vent
Hors des deux tuyaux prompt à s'exhaler avant
Qu'il disperse le son dans une pluie aride,
C'est, à l'horizon pas remué d'une ride,
Le visible et serein souffle artificiel
De l'inspiration, qui regagne le ciel.

THE AFTERNOON OF A FAUN

Eclogue

THE FAUN

I would perpetuate these nymphs.

                            So clear,
their light carnation, that it drifts on the air
drowsy with tufted slumbers.

                            So I loved a dream?
My doubt, a mass of ancient night, concludes
in many a subtle branch, which, since the real woods
remain, proves, alas! what I offered to myself
as triumph was the ideal lack of roses.
Let's think it over . . .

                            if those girls whom you explain
be but an itching in your fabulous brain!
Faun, the illusion escapes from the blue eyes
and cold of the more chaste, like a weeping spring:
but the other one, all sighs, you say, contrasts
like a day-breeze warm upon your fleece!
But no! through the immobile and heavy swoon
stifling with heat the cool morning if it resists,
murmurs no water but that poured from my flute
on the grove sprinkled with harmonies; the only wind
prompt to exhale from the twin-pipes before
it can disperse the sound in an arid rain,
is, on the horizon unstirred by a wrinkle,
the visible and serene artificial breath
of inspiration, which regains the sky.

O bords siciliens d'un calme marécage
Qu'à l'envi des soleils ma vanité saccage,
Tacite sous les fleurs d'étincelles, CONTEZ
"Que je coupais ici les creux roseaux domptés
Par le talent; quand, sur l'or glauque de lointaines
Verdures dédiant leur vigne à des fontaines,
Ondoie une blancheur animale au repos:
Et qu'au prélude lent où naissent les pipeaux
Ce vol de cygnes, non! de naïades se sauve
Ou plonge..."

                  Inerte, tout brûle dans l'heure fauve
Sans marquer par quel art ensemble détala
Trop d'hymen souhaité de qui cherche le *la*:
Alors m'éveillerai-je à la ferveur première,
Droit et seul, sous un flot antique de lumière,
Lys! et l'un de vous tous pour l'ingénuité.

Autre que ce doux rien par leur lèvre ébruité,
Le baiser, qui tout bas des perfides assure,
Mon sein, vierge de preuve, atteste une morsure
Mystérieuse, due à quelque auguste dent;
Mais, bast! arcane tel élut pour confident
Le jonc vaste et jumeau dont sous l'azur on joue:
Qui, détournant à soi le trouble de la joue
Rêve, dans un solo long, que nous amusions
La beauté d'alentour pas des confusions
Fausses entre elle-même et notre chant crédule;
Et de faire aussi haut que l'amour se module
Évanouir du songe ordinaire de dos
Ou de flanc pur suivis avec mes regards clos,
Une sonore, vaine et monotone ligne.

Tâche donc, instrument des fuites, ô maligne
Syrinx, de refleurir aux lacs où tu m'attends!
Moi, de ma rumeur fier, je vais parler longtemps
Des déesses; et par d'idolâtres peintures,
A leur ombre enlever encore des ceintures:

O Sicilian borders of a peaceful marsh
which like unto the sun my vanity plunders,
tacit under the flowers of sparks, RELATE
"How I was cutting here the hollow reeds
tamed by my talent; when, on the glaucous gold
of distant verdures dedicating their vines
to the fountains, undulated an animal whiteness,
reposing: and to the slow prelude whence the pipes
are born, this flight of swans, no! of Naiades
goes scampering off or dives . . ."

                            Inert, all things
burn in the tawny hour, not noticing
by what art together fled this too much hymen
desired by who seeks for *la*: then I'll awaken
to the primal fervor, erect and alone,
under the antique flood of light, O lilies!
and the one among you all for artlessness.

Besides this sweet nothing by their lips made known,
the kiss, that reveals, though hushed, some faithless ones,
my breast, virgin of proof, vouches a bite,
mysterious, from some illustrious tooth;
but enough! as confidant such arcanum chose
the great twin-reeds one plays beneath the azure:
which, diverting to themselves the cheeks' excitement,
dream, in a long solo, that we may amuse
the beauties hereabout by false confusions
between them even and our credulous song;
and to make as high as love can modulate
vanish from the banal dream of backs
or pure flanks pursued in my closed eyes,
a sonorous and vain, monotonous line.

Try then, instrument of flights, O evil
Syrinx, to flower again by the lakes where you wait!
Proud of my noise, I am going to talk at length
of the goddesses; and by idolatrous paintings
to lift again the cinctures from their shadows:

Ainsi, quand des raisins j'ai sucé la clarté,
Pour bannir un regret par ma feinte écarté,
Rieur, j'élève au ciel d'été la grappe vide
Et, soufflant dans ses peaux lumineuses, avide
D'ivresse, jusqu'au soir je regarde au travers.

O nymphes, regonflons des SOUVENIRS divers.
"Mon œil, trouant les joncs, dardait chaque encolure
Immortelle, qui noie en l'onde sa brûlure
Avec un cri de rage au ciel de la forêt;
Et le splendide bain de cheveux disparaît
Dans les clartés et les frissons, ô pierreries!
J'accours; quand, à mes pieds, s'entrejoignent (meurtries
De la langueur goûtée à ce mal d'être deux)
Des dormeuses parmi leurs seuls bras hasardeux;
Je les ravis, sans les désenlacer, et vole
A ce massif, haï par l'ombrage frivole,
De roses tarissant tout parfum au soleil,
Où notre ébat au jour consumé soit pareil."
Je t'adore, courroux des vierges, ô délice
Farouche du sacré fardeau nu qui se glisse
Pour fuir ma lèvre en feu buvant, comme un éclair
Tressaille! le frayeur secrète de la chair:
Des pieds de l'inhumaine au cœur de la timide
Que délaisse à la fois une innocence, humide
De larmes folles ou de moins tristes vapeurs.
"Mon crime, c'est d'avoir, gai de vaincre ces peurs
Traîtresses, divisé la touffe échevelée
De baisers que les dieux gardaient si bien mêlée:
Car, à peine j'allais cacher un rire ardent
Sous les replis heureux d'une seule (gardant
Par un doigt simple, afin que sa candeur de plume
Se teignît à l'émoi de sa sœur qui s'allume,
La petite, naïve et ne rougissant pas:)
Que de mes bras, défaits par de vagues trépas,
Cette proie, à jamais ingrate se délivre
Sans pitié du sanglot dont j'étais encore ivre."

so, when I have sucked the bright juice of the grapes,
to banish a regret by my pretense discarded,
laughing, I raise to the summer sky the empty
hulls and, puffing into these luminous skins,
craving drunkenness, I gaze through them till evening.

O nymphs, we swell with divers MEMORIES.
"Piercing the reeds, my eyes speared each immortal
neck, that drowns its burning in the water
with a cry of rage flung to the forest sky;
and the splendid bath of tresses disappeared
in shimmerings and shiverings, O jewels!
I rush up; when, at my feet, entwine (bruised
by the languor drunk from this harm of being two)
girls sleeping in each other's perilous arms;
I seize them, not untangling them, and run
to this clump, hated by the frivolous shade,
of roses exhausting all their scent in the sun,
where our frolic should be like a squandered day."
I adore you, anger of virgins, O fierce delight
of the sacred naked burden that slips to flee
the fiery drinking of my lips, like the crack
of lightning! the secret terror of the flesh:
from the feet of the heartless one to the heart of the timid
abandoned at the same time by an innocence, humid
with foolish tears or less melancholy vapors.
"My crime is, gay at vanquishing their traitress
fears, to have parted the disheveled tangle
of kisses that the gods kept so well mingled;
for I was just going to hide a glowing laugh
in the happy creases of one (even while I kept
with only a finger—so that her plume's candor
should be stained by the frenzy of her sister
who burned—the little one, naïve, not blushing a bit:)
when from my arms, relaxed by the vague death,
this prey, forever ungrateful, frees itself,
not pitying the sob that still bedrunkened me."

Tant pis! vers le bonheur d'autres m'entraîneront
Par leur tresse nouée aux cornes de mon front:
Tu sais, ma passion, que, pourpre et déjà mûre,
Chaque grenade éclate et d'abeilles murmure;
Et notre sang, épris de qui le va saisir,
Coule pour tout l'essaim éternel du désir.
A l'heure où ce bois d'or et de cendres se teinte
Une fête s'exalte en la feuillée éteinte:
Etna! c'est parmi toi visité de Vénus
Sur ta lave posant ses talons ingénus,
Quand tonne un somme triste ou s'épuise la flamme.
Je tiens la reine!

       O sûr châtiment...

                Non, mais l'âme
De paroles vacante et ce corps alourdi
Tard succombent au fier silence de midi:
Sans plus il faut dormir en l'oubli du blasphème,
Sur le sable altéré gisant et comme j'aime
Ouvrir ma bouche à l'astre efficace des vins!

Couple, adieu; je vais voir l'ombre que tu devins.

Too bad! but others will lead me toward happiness,
knotting the horns on my brow with many a tress;
you know, my passion, how, crimson and already ripe,
every pomegranate bursts and murmurs with bees;
and our blood, burning for who is going to receive it,
flows for all the eternal swarm of desire.
At the hour when this wood is stained with gold and ashes
a feast exults among extinguished leaves:
Etna! it is on you visited by Venus
upon your lava setting her candid feet
when thunders a sad slumber or the flame expires.
I embrace the queen!

        Sure punishment . . .

                      No, but the spirit
empty of words now and the body numbed
unto noon's haughty silence at last succumb:
enough! on the thirsty sand, forgetful of
the outrage, I must sleep, and as I love
open my mouth to the powerful star of wine!

Sweet pair, farewell. I shall see the shades you became.

SAINTE

A la fenêtre recélant
Le santal vieux qui se dédore
De sa viole étincelant
Jadis avec flûte ou mandore,

Est la Sainte pâle, étalant
Le livre vieux qui se déplie
Du Magnificat ruisselant
Jadis selon vêpre et complie:

A ce vitrage d'ostensoir
Que frôle une harpe par l'Ange
Formée avec son vol du soir
Pour la délicate phalange

Du doigt que, sans le vieux santal
Ni le vieux livre, elle balance,
Sur le plumage instrumental,
Musicienne du silence.

SAINT

At the window concealing
the old sandalwood lute
that once, its gilt is peeling,
shone with mandora or flute,

is the pale Saint, showing
the old book outspread
at the Magnificat glowing
once for services read;

at this stained-glass window lightly
touched by a harp shaped
by the Angel in evening flight
for the delicate finger-tip

that, without the old santal
or the old book, she balances
on the plumage instrumental,
musician of silence.

PROSE

pour des Esseintes

Hyperbole! de ma mémoire
Triomphalement ne sais-tu
Te lever, aujourd'hui grimoire
Dans un livre de fer vêtu:

Car j'installe, par la science,
L'hymne des cœurs spirituels
En l'œuvre de ma patience,
Atlas, herbiers et rituels.

Nous promenions notre visage
(Nous fûmes deux, je le maintiens)
Sur maints charmes de paysage,
O sœur, y comparant les tiens.

L'ère d'autorité se trouble
Lorsque, sans nul motif, on dit
De ce midi que notre double
Inconscience approfondit

Que, sol des cent iris, son site,
Ils savent s'il a bien été,
Ne porte pas de nom que cite
L'or de la trompette d'Été.

Oui, dans une île que l'air charge
De vue et non de visions
Toute fleur s'étalait plus large
Sans que nous en devisions.

PROSE

for Des Esseintes

Hyperbole! from my memory
triumphant can you not arise,
today from a book bound with iron
as cabalistic gramaries:

because by knowledge I induct
the hymn of all hearts spirituel
to this labor of my patience,
atlas, herbal, ritual.

We would turn our visages
(I maintain that we were two),
O sister, to the landscape's charms,
always comparing them with you.

The era of authority
is troubled when, with no motifs,
they say of this southland our double
mind's subconsciousness perceives

that, hundred-iris bed, its site,
they know if really it existed,
does not bear a name the gold
of the Summer's trumpet cited.

Yes, on an island charged by air
not with visions but with sight
every flower showed off, freer,
though we never spoke of it.

Telles, immenses, que chacune
Ordinairement se para
D'un lucide contour, lacune
Qui des jardins la sépara.

Gloire du long désir, Idées
Tout en moi s'exaltait de voir
La famille des iridées
Surgir à ce nouveau devoir,

Mais cette sœur sensée et tendre
Ne porta son regard plus loin
Que sourire et, comme à l'entendre
J'occupe mon antique soin.

Oh! sache l'Esprit de litige,
A cette heure où nous nous taisons,
Que de lits multiples la tige
Grandissait trop pour nos raisons

Et non comme pleure la rive,
Quand son jeu monotone ment
A vouloir que l'ampleur arrive
Parmi mon jeune étonnement

D'ouïr tout le ciel et la carte
Sans fin attestés sur mes pas,
Par le flot même qui s'écarte,
Que ce pays n'exista pas.

L'enfant abdique son extase
Et docte déjà par chemins
Elle dit le mot: Anastase!
Né pour d'éternels parchemins,

Avant qu'un sépulcre ne rie
Sous aucun climat, son aïeul,
De porter ce nom: Pulchérie!
Caché par le trop grand glaïeul.

Such, immense, that every one
usually adorned itself
with a lucid edge, lacuna
which from the gardens set it off.

Glory of long desire, Ideas
all in me with great elation
saw the family Irides
arise to this new consecration,

but this sensible fond sister
went no further than to spare
a smile and, to understand her,
I attend my ancient care.

O Spirit of contention! know
at this hour when we are still,
that too tall for reason grows
the stalk of multiple asphodels

and not as the shore weeps,
when its monotonous frolic lies
to wish an amplitude would come
into my juvenile surprise

at hearing all the sky and map
always in my steps attested,
by the wave even that ebbs away,
that this country never existed.

Already lessoned by the roads
the child resigns her ecstasy
and says it: Anastasius! born
for parchments of eternity,

before a sepulcher could laugh
in any clime, her ancestor,
to bear the name: Pulcheria!
hidden by the too great lily's flower.

AUTRE ÉVENTAIL

de Mademoiselle Mallarmé

O rêveuse, pour que je plonge
Au pur délice sans chemin,
Sache, par un subtil mensonge,
Garder mon aile dans ta main.

Une fraîcheur de crépuscule
Te vient à chaque battement
Dont le coup prisonnier recule
L'horizon délicatement.

Vertige! voici que frissonne
L'espace comme un grand baiser
Qui, fou de naître pour personne,
Ne peut jaillir ni s'apaiser.

Sens-tu le paradis farouche
Ainsi qu'un rire enseveli
Se couler du coin de ta bouche
Au fond de l'unanime pli!

Le sceptre des rivages roses
Stagnants sur les soirs d'or, ce l'est,
Ce blanc vol fermé que tu poses
Contre le feu d'un bracelet.

ANOTHER FAN

of Mademoiselle Mallarmé

O dreamer, that I may dive
in pure pathless delight, understand
how subtly to connive
to keep my wing in your hand.

A coolness of twilight is sent
over you by each imprisoned
flutter whose beat extends
delicately the horizon.

Vertigo! how space quakes
like a great kiss, wild
to be born for no one's sake,
but can neither spring forth nor be stilled.

Do you feel the fierce paradise
like stifled laughter that slips
from the corner of your lips
to the deep unanimous crease?

The scepter of shores of rose
stagnant on evenings of gold, it's
this white closed flight you pose
against the fire of a bracelet.

LE TOMBEAU DE CHARLES BAUDELAIRE

Le temple enseveli divulgue par la bouche
Sépulcrale d'égout bavant boue et rubis
Abominablement quelque idole Anubis
Tout le museau flambé comme un aboi farouche

Ou que le gaz récent torde la mèche louche
Essuyeuse on le sait des opprobres subis
Il allume hagard un immortel pubis
Dont le vol selon le réverbère découche

Quel feuillage séché dans les cités sans soir
Votif pourra bénir comme elle se rasseoir
Contre le marbre vainement de Baudelaire

Au voile qui la ceint absente avec frissons
Celle son Ombre même un poison tutélaire
Toujours à respirer si nous en périssons.

THE TOMB OF CHARLES BAUDELAIRE

The buried temple reveals by the sewer's dark
sepulchral mouth slavering mud and rubies
abominably some idol of Anubis
all the muzzle flaming like a ferocious bark

or if the recent gas twists a squirming wick
that puts up with who knows what dubious
disgrace it haggardly lights an immortal pubis
whose flight depends on the streetlamp to stay awake

What dried wreaths in cities without evening
votively could bless as if could sit
vainly against the marble of Baudelaire

(in the veil that clothes the absent with shudderings)
this his Shade even a poison tutelar
ever to be breathed though we die of it.

MES BOUQUINS...

Mes bouquins refermés sur le nom de Paphos,
Il m'amuse d'élire avec le seul génie
Une ruine, par mille écumes bénie
Sous l'hyacinthe, au loin, de ses jours triomphaux.

Coure le froid avec ses silences de faux,
Je n'y hululerai pas de vide nénie
Si ce très blanc ébat au ras du sol dénie
A tout site l'honneur du paysage faux.

Ma faim qui d'aucuns fruits ici ne se régale
Trouve en leur docte manque une saveur égale:
Qu'un éclate de chair humain et parfumant!

Le pied sur quelque givre où notre amour tisonne,
Je pense plus longtemps peut-être éperdument
A l'autre, au sein brûlé d'une antique amazone.

MY OLD BOOKS . . .

My old books closed on Paphos' name, I elect
at the whim of the one genius, far away,
a ruin, blessed by a thousand foamy flecks
under hyacinth, in its triumphal days.

Let the cold run with its silences of scythes,
I shall not ululate here an empty wail
if this very white frolic skimming the ground denies
to any landscape the honor of being unreal.

My hunger that will feast on no fruits here
finds in their learned lack an equal taste:
although this fragrant human flesh should burst!

Feet on some wyvern where our love stirs the fire,
longer perhaps distracted I brood on
the other, with seared breast of an ancient Amazon.

Arthur Rimbaud

LE DORMEUR DU VAL

C'est un trou de verdure où chante une rivière
Accrochant follement aux herbes des haillons
D'argent; où le soleil, de la montagne fière,
Luit: c'est un petit val qui mousse de rayons.

Un soldat jeune, bouche ouverte, tête nue,
Et la nuque baignant dans la frais cresson bleu,
Dort; il est étendu dans l'herbe, sous la nue,
Pâle dans son lit vert où la lumière pleut.

Les pieds dans les glaïeuls, il dort. Souriant comme
Sourirait un enfant malade, il fait un somme:
Nature, berce-le chaudement: il a froid.

Les parfums ne font pas frissonner sa narine;
Il dort dans le soleil, la main sur sa poitrine
Tranquille. Il a deux trous rouges au côté droit.

THE SLEEPER IN THE VALLEY

There's a green trough where a singing river
clings crazily to tattered grass that gleams
with silver, where from the proud mountain shivers
sunlight, and the valley foams with beams.

A soldier, young, with open mouth, bare head;
his neck is bathed in cool blue watercress;
under high clouds he sleeps, stretched on the grass,
and light rains on him, pale in his green bed.

He sleeps, his feet in irises. His smile
is like a sick child's, as he naps a while.
Nature, cradle him snugly; he is cold!

The fragrance wakens no quiver in his nostrils;
hand on his breast, he sleeps in sunlight, tranquil.
In his right side there are two red holes.

LES CHERCHEUSES DE POUX

Quand le front de l'enfant, plein de rouges tourmentes,
Implore l'essaim blanc des rêves indistincts,
Il vient près de son lit deux grandes sœurs charmantes
Avec de frêles doigts aux ongles argentins.

Elles assoient l'enfant devant une croisée
Grande ouverte où l'air bleu baigne un fouillis de fleurs,
Et dans ses lourds cheveux où tombe la rosée
Promènent leurs doigts fins, terribles et charmeurs.

Il écoute chanter leurs haleines craintives
Qui fleurent de longs miels végétaux et rosés,
Et qu'interrompt parfois un sifflement, salives
Reprises sur la lèvre ou désirs de baisers.

Il entend leurs cils noirs battant sous les silences
Parfumés; et leurs doigts électriques et doux
Font crépiter parmi ses grises indolences
Sous leurs ongles royaux la mort des petits poux.

Voilà que monte en lui le vin de la Paresse,
Soupir d'harmonica qui pourrait délirer;
L'enfant se sent, selon la lenteur des caresses,
Sourdre et mourir sans cesse un désir de pleurer.

THE LICE-HUNTERS

When the child's forehead, covered with the red
torment, begs the dream-swarm, vague and pale,
two tall gracious nuns come to his bed,
with delicate hands and silvery fingernails.

They seat the child by the open window where
blue atmosphere is bathing a flowery tangle,
and as the dew settles on his mop of hair,
dreadful and charming, the shrewd fingers ramble.

He hears their timid breathing sing, whence slips
a vegetable rose-nectar that by hisses
is sometimes interrupted, as when lips
suck back saliva or the desire for kisses.

He hears the blinking of their black eyelashes
in the perfumed stillness and, as in a vise,
royal nails electrically mashing
to crackling death the gray and lazy lice.

Then works in him the wine of Idleness,
the delirium of a mouth-organ's sigh:
and the child feels, under the slow caresses,
welling and sinking an endless need to cry.

LE BATEAU IVRE

Comme je descendais des Fleuves impassibles,
Je ne me sentis plus guidé par les haleurs:
Des Peaux-Rouges criards les avaient pris pour cibles,
Les ayant cloués nus aux poteaux de couleurs.

J'étais insoucieux de tous les équipages,
Porteur de blés flamands ou de cotons anglais.
Quand avec mes haleurs ont fini ces tapages,
Les Fleuves m'ont laissé descendre où je voulais.

Dans les clapotements furieux des marées,
Moi, l'autre hiver, plus sourd que les cerveaux d'enfants,
Je courus! Et les Péninsules démarrées
N'ont pas subi tohu-bohus plus triomphants.

La tempête a béni mes éveils maritimes.
Plus léger qu'un bouchon j'ai dansé sur les flots
Qu'on appelle rouleurs éternels de victimes,
Dix nuits, sans regretter l'œil niais des falots!

Plus douce qu'aux enfants la chair des pommes sures,
L'eau verte pénétra ma coque de sapin
Et des taches de vins bleus et des vomissures
Me lava, dispersant gouvernail et grappin.

Et dès lors, je me suis baigné dans le Poème
De la Mer, infusé d'astres, et lactescent,
Dévorant les azurs verts; où, flottaison blême
Et ravie, un noyé pensif parfois descend;

THE DRUNKEN BOAT

As I was going down the impassive Rivers,
I felt no longer guided by the haulers;
the yelling Redskins were emptying their quivers
at them, nailed naked to stakes of various colors.

Transporter of English cottons and Flemish grain,
I was a bit negligent about the crew,
and when my haulers had finished their hullabaloo,
the Rivers let me go where I wished again.

In the furious waters' smacks and rumbles,
last winter, duller than a baby's brains,
I ran! and the Peninsulas, slipping their chains,
never underwent such triumphant jumbles.

The tempest blessed my maritime awakings.
Lighter than cork, ten nights did I dance there
on the rollers, called the eternal victim-breakers,
without regretting the lanterns' silly stare.

Sweeter than the flesh of sour apples
to a child, green water pierced my cockle of pine,
cleaned me of vomit and blue stains of wine,
losing also the rudder and the grapple.

Since then, I am bathed in the Poem of the Ocean,
the sea lactescent and infused with stars,
devouring the azure-green where, pale flotation,
and ravished, a drowned pensive one sinks far;

Où, teignant tout à coup les bleuités, délires
Et rythmes lents sous les rutilements du jour,
Plus fortes que l'alcool, plus vastes que nos lyres,
Fermentent les rousseurs amères de l'amour!

Je sais les cieux crevant en éclairs, et les trombes
Et les ressacs et les courants: je sais le soir,
L'Aube exaltée ainsi qu'un peuple de colombes,
Et j'ai vu quelquefois ce que l'homme a cru voir!

J'ai vu le soleil bas, taché d'horreurs mystiques,
Illuminant de longs figements violets,
Pareils à des acteurs de drames très-antiques
Les flots roulant au loin leurs frissons de volets!

J'ai rêvé la nuit verte aux neiges éblouies,
Baiser montant aux yeux des mers avec lenteurs,
La circulation des sèves inouïes,
Et l'éveil jaune et bleu des phosphores chanteurs!

J'ai suivi, des mois pleins, pareille aux vacheries
Hystériques, la houle à l'assaut des récifs,
Sans songer que les pieds lumineux des Maries
Pussent forcer le mufle aux Océans poussifs!

J'ai heurté, savez-vous, d'incroyables Florides
Mêlant aux fleurs des yeux de panthères à peaux
D'hommes! Des arcs-en-ciel tendus comme des brides
Sous l'horizon des mers, à de glauques troupeaux!

J'ai vu fermenter les marais énormes, nasses
Où pourrit dans les joncs tout un Léviathan!
Des écroulements d'eaux au milieu des bonaces,
Et les lointains vers les gouffres cataractant!

where, suddenly staining the blues, delirious fires
and rhythms slow beneath day's rutilance,
stronger than alcohol, vaster than our lyres,
the bitter maculae of love ferment.

I know the lightning-riven skies, the waves,
the waterspouts and tides; I know the night,
and the dawn exalted, as with a flock of doves,
and have sometimes seen what man thinks meets his sight.

I've seen the low sun, stained by mysteries
of horror, lighting with long purple clots
like actors in the ancient tragedies
waves rolling far their flicker of shutter-slats.

I have dreamed the green night with bedazzled snow,
kisses that rise to the iris of the sea,
the marvelous ichors' circulatory flow
and phosphorous singing its green reveille.

I've followed, like tricks of maddened cows, the beat
of waves on reefs, for months, but hadn't a notion
that they could be muzzled by the luminous feet
of the Marys, silencing the wheezy Oceans.

I've jostled improbable Floridas, you know,
mingling flowers and eyes of panthers with human hides;
rainbows stretched like bridle-reins below
the sea's horizon, to the glaucous herds.

I've seen the swamps ferment, enormous meshes
of traps where Leviathan rotted among the rushes,
where in the midst of calms the water crashes,
and the distances cataracting toward the abysses.

Glaciers, soleils d'argent, flots nacreux, cieux de braises!
Échouages hideux au fond des golfes bruns
Où les serpents géants dévorés des punaises
Choient, des arbres tordus, avec de noirs parfums!

J'aurais voulu montrer aux enfants ces dorades
Du flot bleu, ces poissons d'or, ces poissons chantants.
—Des écumes de fleurs ont bercé mes dérades
Et d'ineffables vents m'ont ailé par instants.

Parfois, martyr lassé des pôles et des zones,
La mer dont le sanglot faisait mon roulis doux
Montait vers moi ses fleurs d'ombre aux ventouses jaunes
Et je restais, ainsi qu'une femme à genoux...

Presque île, ballottant sur mes bords les querelles
Et les fientes d'oiseaux clabaudeurs aux yeux blonds.
Et je voguais, lorsqu'à travers mes liens frêles
Des noyés descendaient dormir, à reculons!...

Or moi, bateau perdu sous les cheveux des anses,
Jeté par l'ouragan dans l'éther sans oiseau,
Moi dont les Monitors et les voiliers des Hanses
N'auraient pas repêché la carcasse ivre d'eau;

Libre, fumant, monté de brumes violettes,
Moi qui trouais le ciel rougeoyant comme un mur
Qui porte, confiture exquise aux bons poètes,
Des lichens de soleil et des morves d'azur;

Qui courais, taché de lunules électriques,
Planche folle, escorté des hippocampes noirs,
Quand les juillets faisaient crouler à coups de triques
Les cieux ultramarins aux ardents entonnoirs;

Glaciers, pearl-waves, hot skies, suns of silver,
hideous strandings in dark gulfs of gloom
where giant serpents, by insects devoured,
fall from twisted trees with black perfumes.

I've had loved to have had the children see
among blue waves these golden fish that sing.
Foam-flowers have lulled me, driven out to sea,
and ineffable winds have given me instant wings.

Sometimes, weary of poles and zones, a martyr
I was rocked by the sobbing rolling of the seas
bringing me ghostly flowers with yellow suckers,
and I stayed there, like a woman on her knees . . .

near-island, tossing over my gunnels the wranglings
and droppings of white-eyed scandal-mongering birds.
And I sailed on until, with my frail lines tangling,
the drowned men drifted down to sleep, backwards . . .

Then I, a boat lost in the weeds of creeks,
hurled by the hurricane in the birdless ether,
I, and no Monitors or Hansa barks
could have fished up my carcass drunken with water;

reeking and free, arisen from fogs of violet,
I who was ripping a hole in the reddening heavens
like a wall that bears—exquisite jam for nice poets—
the phlegm of azure and the sunlight's lichens;

I was running, spotted with electric lunules,
a crazy plank, with black seahorses cruising,
when the Julys with bludgeon blows were crushing
the skies of ultramarine with fiery funnels;

Moi qui tremblais, sentant geindre à cinquante lieues
Le rut des Béhémots et les Maelstroms épais,
Fileur éternel des immobilités bleues,
Je regrette l'Europe aux anciens parapets!

J'ai vu des archipels sidéraux! et des îles
Dont les cieux délirants sont ouverts au vogueur:
—Est-ce en ces nuits sans fonds que tu dors et t'exiles,
Million d'oiseaux d'or, ô future Vigueur?—

Mais, vrai, j'ai trop pleuré! Les Aubes sont navrantes.
Toute lune est atroce et tout soleil amer:
L'âcre amour m'a gonflé de torpeurs enivrantes.
O que ma quille éclate! O que j'aille à la mer!

Si je désire une eau d'Europe, c'est la flache
Noire et froide où vers le crépuscule embaumé
Un enfant accroupi plein de tristesses, lâche
Un bateau frêle comme un papillon de mai.

Je ne puis plus, baigné de vos langueurs, ô lames,
Enlever leur sillage aux porteurs de cotons,
Ni traverser l'orgueil des drapeaux et des flammes,
Ni nager sous les yeux horribles des pontons.

great Behemoth's ruts, the Maelstrom's brawls,
heard fifty leagues away, have made me shiver,
spinner of blue immobilities forever;
I hanker for Europe with its ancient walls.

I've seen star-archipelagoes! and isles
with frenzied skies wide open to the voyager:
do you sleep through endless nights of self-exile,
a million golden birds, O future Vigor?

But really I've wept too much. Dawns make me suffer,
all moons are vile, all suns are gall to me.
Harsh love has bloated me with drunken torpors.
Oh, let my keel shiver! Oh, let me go down to the sea!

If I want any water of Europe, it's a slough,
black and cold, at the fragrant close of day,
where, squatting, a sad child launches his new
sailboat, frail as a butterfly of May.

No longer, billows, bathing in your languors,
can I overhaul the cotton-freighters' wakes,
or make my way through the pride of pennants and banners,
or sail before the horrible eyes of the hulks.

COMPLAINTE DES PIANOS
QU'ON ENTEND DANS LES QUARTIERS AISÉS

Menez l'âme que les Lettres ont bien nourrie,
Les pianos, les pianos, dans les quartiers aisés!
Premiers soirs, sans pardessus, chaste flânerie,
Aux complaintes des nerfs incompris ou brisés.

    Ces enfants, à quoi rêvent-elles,
    Dans les ennuis des ritournelles?

        —"Préaux des soirs,
        Christs des dortoirs!

  "Tu t'en vas et tu nous laisses,
    Tu nous laiss's et tu t'en vas,
    Défaire et refaire ses tresses,
    Broder d'éternels canevas."

Jolie ou vague? triste ou sage? encore pure?
O jours, tout m'est égal? ou, monde, moi je veux?
Et si vierge, du moins, de la bonne blessure,
Sachant quels gras couchants ont les plus blancs aveux?

    Mon Dieu, à quoi donc rêvent-elles?
    A des Roland, à des dentelles?

        —"Cœurs en prison,
        Lentes saisons!

  "Tu t'en vas et tu nous quittes,
    Tu nous quitt's et tu t'en vas!
    Couvents gris, chœurs de Sulamites,
    Sur nos seins nuls croisons nos bras."

COMPLAINT OF THE PIANOS
ONE HEARS IN THE BETTER NEIGHBORHOODS

A soul fed on belles-lettres, for such a soul—
the pianos, pianos, in the better neighborhoods!—
late afternoons, no topcoat, a chaste stroll;
it's shattered with nervous disorders not understood.

These young girls, what dreamy spells
in the boredom of the ritornelles?

—"Walks in evening's glories,
Christs of the dormitories!

"You go away and leave us here,
you leave us and go off as you please,
we can take down ond put up our hair,
and do eternal embroideries."

Pretty or hazy? still pure? sad or profound?
O days, do I care? World, what do I want now?
And so virginal, at least, of that kindly wound,
knowing what fat sunsets have the whitest vows?

God, what do they dream in these places?
About some Roland? About laces?

—"Hearts in prison,
languid seasons!

"You leave us alone, you go away,
you go away and we're by-passed!
Chorus of Shulamites, nunneries gray,
we cross our arms on our absent breasts."

Fatales clés de l'être un beau jour apparues;
Psitt! aux hérédités en ponctuels ferments,
Dans le bal incessant de nos étranges rues;
Ah! pensionnats, théâtres, journaux, romans!

Allez, stériles ritournelles,
La vie est vraie et criminelle.

—"Rideaux tirés,
Peut-on entrer?

"Tu t'en vas et tu nous laisses,
Tu nous laiss's et tu t'en vas,
La source des frais rosiers baisse,
Vraiment! Et lui qui ne vient pas... "

Il viendra! Vous serez les pauvres cœurs en faute,
Fiancés au remords comme aux essais sans fond,
Et les suffisants cœurs cossus, n'ayant d'autre hôte
Qu'un train-train pavoisé d'estime et de chiffons.

Mourir? peut-être brodent-elles,
Pour un oncle à dot, des bretelles?

—"Jamais! Jamais!
Si tu savais!

"Tu t'en vas et tu nous quittes,
Tu nous quitt's et tu t'en vas,
Mais tu nous reviendras bien vite
Guérir mon beau mal, n'est-ce pas?"

Et c'est vrai! l'Idéal les faits divaguer toutes,
Vigne bohême, même en ces quartiers aisés.
La vie est là; le pur flacon des vives gouttes
Sera, *comme il convient,* d'eau propre baptisé.

Inevitable signs that we'll have good weather;
pfft! with successions of punctual upheavals,
in our crazy streets the ball goes on forever;
ah, the day-schools, theaters, newspapers, and novels!

Enough of you, dead ritornelles!
Life is true and criminal.

—"Curtains drawn,
perhaps someone?

"You go and leave us as you please,
you leave us and you go alone,
the fountain fails the fresh rose-trees,
really! And he who doesn't come . . ."

He'll come! You'll have your poor and erring breast
betrothed to remorses and attempts based on
nothing; your rich spoiled heart with no other guest
than boredom decked with self-esteem and chiffon.

Die? Perhaps they embroider flowery
braces for uncles who'll give a dowry?

—"Never! never! You,
if you only knew!

"You go away and leave us here,
you leave us and away you go,
but you'll come soon again to cure
our lovely troubles, isn't it so?"

It's true! The Ideal upsets the verities,
a wandering vine, even in these affluent quarters.
There's life here: the pure vase, *when he agrees*,
will be baptized with virile and proper water.

Aussi, bientôt, se joueront-elles
De plus exactes ritournelles.

—"Seul oreiller!
Mur familier!

"Tu t'en vas et tu nous laisses,
Tu nous laiss's et tu t'en vas.
Que ne suis-je morte à la messe!
Ô mois, ô linges, ô repas!"

Rue Madame.

COMPLAINTE
DE L'OUBLI DES MORTS

Mesdames et Messieurs,
Vous dont la mère est morte,
C'est le bon fossoyeux
Qui gratte à votre porte.

Les morts
C'est sous terre;
Ça n'en sort
Guère.

Vous fumez dans vos bocks,
Vous soldez quelque idylle,
Là-bas chante le coq,
Pauvres morts hors des villes!

Also, soon will disport themselves
the most correct of ritornelles.

    —"Pillow alone!
    Wall well-known!

"You go away and leave us, alas,
 you go and leave us unappeased.
 If only I don't die at Mass!
 O months! O linens! O wedding feasts!"

Rue Madame.

COMPLAINT

OF NEGLECTING THE DEAD

Ladies and Gentlemen,
you whose mother has died,
that's the gravedigger again,
scratching there, outside.

    The dead lie low
    underground;
    they don't go
    much around.

You smoke and drink your bock,
settle some old affair,
yonder crows the cock,
poor dead folks out there!

Grand-papa se penchait,
Là, le doigt sur la tempe,
Sœur faisait du crochet,
Mère montait la lampe.

Les morts
C'est discret,
Ça dort
Trop au frais.

Vous avez bien diné,
Comment va cette affaire?
Ah! les petits mort-nés
Ne se dorlotent guère!

Notez, d'un trait égal,
Au livre de la caisse,
Entre deux frais de bal:
Entretien tombe et messe.

C'est gai,
Cette vie;
Hein, ma mie,
O gué?

Mesdames et Messieurs,
Vous dont la sœur est morte,
Ouvrez au fossoyeux
Qui claque à votre porte;

Si vous n'avez pitié,
Il viendra (sans rancune)
Vous tirer par les pieds,
Une nuit de grand'lune!

Importun
Vent qui rage!
Les défunts?
Ça voyage...

Finger at his brow,
that's old Gramp,
Sister crochets, now
Ma trims up the lamp.

> The dead keep
> silent, really
> their sleep
> is too chilly.

Did you dine well? Did
that sharp deal pan out?
Ah, those stillborn kids
don't indulge a lot!

In the expense account
among the balls you gave
enter the amount
for masses and your grave.

> It's a gay
> life here!
> Eh, dear,
> what say?

Ladies and Gentlemen,
you whose sister died,
open the door again,
the sexton knocks outside.

He'll come if you don't feel
pity; without spite,
will drag you by the heels
one full moonlight night!

> The mad
> winds whip!
> The dead?
> Quite a trip . . .

DIMANCHES

Le ciel pleut sans but, sans que rien l'émeuve,
Il pleut, il pleut, bergère! sur le fleuve...

Le fleuve a son repos dominical;
Pas un chaland, en amont, en aval.

Les Vêpres carillonnent sur la ville.
Les berges sont désertes, sans idylles.

Passe un pensionnat (ô pauvres chairs!)
Plusieurs ont déjà leurs manchons d'hiver.

Une qui n'a ni manchon, ni fourrures
Fait, tout en gris, une pauvre figure.

Et la voilà qui s'échappe des rangs,
Et court? ô mon Dieu, qu'est-ce qu'il lui prend?

Et elle va se jeter dans le fleuve.
Pas un batelier, pas un chien Terr'-Neuve.

Le crépuscule vient; le petit port
Allume ses feux. (Ah! connu, l' décor!).

La pluie continue à mouiller le fleuve,
Le ciel pleut sans but, sans que rien l'émeuve.

SUNDAYS

The sky keeps raining, with no cause whatever,
shepherdess, it rains and rains on the river . . .

Not a barge upstream or down, the river flows
tranquilly in its Sabbath Day repose.

Deserted banks. No idylls. On the town
the vesper carillons are drifting down.

A group from a boarding school (poor creatures!) goes
already with their muffs and winter clothes.

One who has neither muff nor furs today
looks pretty pathetic in her somber gray.

Then suddenly—see there!—she darts from the ranks
and runs—My God! is she crazy?—to the bank.

She's going to throw herself in the water, and there
isn't a boatman or Newfoundland dog anywhere.

Now twilight falls. The little port once more
kindles its fires. (Ah, the well-known décor!)

The rain continues to wet down the river,
the sky keeps raining, with no cause whatever.

LAFORGUE   97

ALBUMS

On m'a dit la vie au Far-West et les Prairies,
Et mon sang a gémi: "Que voilà ma patrie!..."
Déclassé du vieux monde, être sans foi ni loi,
Desperado! là-bas, là-bas, je serai roi!...
Oh! là-bas, m'y scalper de mon cerveau d'Europe!
Piaffer, redevenir une vierge antilope,
Sans littérature, un gars de proie, citoyen
Du hasard et sifflant l'argot californien!
Un colon vague et pur, éleveur, architecte,
Chasseur, pêcheur, joueur, au-dessus des Pandectes!
Entre la mer, et les États Mormons! Des venaisons
Et du whisky! vêtu de cuir, et le gazon
Des Prairies pour lit, et des ciels des premiers âges
Riches comme des corbeilles de mariage!....
Et puis quoi? De bivouac en bivouac, et la Loi
De Lynch; et aujourd'hui des diamants bruts aux doigts,
Et ce soir nuit de jeu, et demain la refuite
Par la Prairie et vers la folie des pépites!...
Et, devenu vieux, la ferme au soleil levant,
Une vache laitière et des petits-enfants...
Et, comme je dessine au besoin, à l'entrée
Je mettrais: "Tatoueur des bras de la contrée!"
Et voilà. Et puis, si mon grand cœur de Paris
Me revenait, chantant: "Oh! pas encor guéri!
"Et ta postérité, pas pour longtemps coureuse!..."
Et si ton vol, Condor des Montagnes-Rocheuses,
Me montrait l'Infini ennemi du confort,
Eh! bien, j'inventerais un culte d'Age d'or,
Un code social, empirique et mystique,
Pour des Peuples Pasteurs modernes et védiques!...

Oh! qu'ils sont beaux les feux de paille! qu'ils sont fous,
Les albums! et non incassables, mes joujoux!...

ALBUMS

I've heard of the Far West, the Prairies, life in the raw,
and my blood groaned: "Would that were my fatherland! . . ."
Cast off by the Old World, without faith or law,
out there I'd be king, a desperado—grand!
Out there I'd scalp myself of my brain from Europe!
To prance, turned to a virgin antelope,
no literature, living by chance, as a roughneck,
wheezing the California dialect!
A genuine rancher, stockman, architect,
hunter, fisherman, gambler, beyond the Pandects!
Between the sea and the Mormons! With venison
and whiskey! clothed in skins, having for bedding
the grass of the Prairies, under the primitive sky,
rich as the baskets of flowers at a wedding! . . .
Then what? Campfire to campfire, Lynch law, the tough
life; today with diamonds in the rough
on my fingers, faro tonight, then tomorrow shrug it
off and dash back to the hills and go nuts after nuggets! . . .
Grown old: a farm that faces the morning sun,
a milch cow and some children,
        and at the entry
a sign on the gate: "Tattooer for the country!"
Just see my arms. Then, if my heart were lured
by Paris, singing: "So! you're not yet cured?
And your children too still gadabouts out yonder!"
And if your flight, O Rocky Mountain Condor,
showed me the Infinite, enemy of content,
oh well, I'd found a religious cult, or invent
a social code, empirical and mystic,
for Pastoral Peoples, a hash of modern and Vedic! . . .

Oh, what fine bonfires of straw! these crazy joys,
these picture-albums, my not unbreakable toys! . . .

NOTRE PETITE COMPAGNE

Si mon air vous dit quelque chose,
Vous auriez tort de vous gêner;
Je ne la fais pas à la pose;
Je suis la Femme, on me connaît.

Bandeaux plats ou crinière folle,
Dites? quel Front vous rendrait fou?
J'ai l'art de toutes les écoles,
J'ai des âmes pour tous les goûts.

Cueillez la fleur de mes visages,
Buvez ma bouche et non ma voix,
Et n'en cherchez pas davantage...
Nul n'y vit clair; pas même moi.

Nos armes ne sont pas égales,
Pour que je vous tende la main,
Vous n'êtes que de naïfs mâles,
Je suis l'Éternel Féminin!

Mon But se perd dans les Étoiles!
C'est moi qui suis la Grande Isis!
Nul ne m'a retroussé mon voile.
Ne songez qu'à mes oasis...

Si mon Air vous dit quelque chose,
Vous auriez tort de vous gêner;
Je ne le fais pas à la pose:
Je suis La Femme! on me connaît.

OUR DEAR LITTLE PARTNER

If my ways appeal to you,
don't be bashful; feel at home.
There's no pose in what I do;
I am Woman, I am known.

My Forehead makes you play the fool?
Wind-blown or with ribbons graced?
I've the arts of every school,
I've a soul for every taste.

Drink my lips and not my voice;
pick my flowers. Do not try
to find more there. You've no choice . . .
none sees clearly here; nor I.

All your weapons won't prevail,
though I put my hand within
yours, you're but the naïf male,
I'm the Eternal Feminine.

Lost among the Stars, my Goal!
I am she, the mighty Isis!
None has pulled aside my veil.
Only dream of my oasis . . .

If my Ways appeal to you,
don't be bashful; feel at home.
There's no pose in what I do;
I am Woman! I am known.

Paul Valéry

HÉLÈNE

Azur! c'est moi... Je viens des grottes de la mort
Entendre l'onde se rompre aux degrés sonores,
Et je revois les galères dans les aurores
Ressusciter de l'ombre au fil des rames d'or.

Mes solitaires mains appellent les monarques
Dont la barbe de sel amusait mes doigts purs;
Je pleurais. Ils chantaient leurs triomphes obscurs
Et les golfes enfuis des poupes de leurs barques.

J'entends les conques profondes et les clairons
Militaires rythmer le vol des avirons;
Le chant clair des rameurs enchaîne le tumulte,

Et les Dieux, à la proue héroïque exaltés,
Dans leur sourire antique et que l'écume insulte,
Tendent vers moi leurs bras indulgents et sculptés.

HELEN

Azure! it's I . . . from the crypts of death I come
to hear the waves break on the resounding stairs,
and I see the galleys once again at dawn
reviving from night on the wake of the golden oars.

My solitary hands call forth the monarchs—
my pure fingers played with those salty beards;
I wept. They were singing of their triumphs obscured
and the buried gulfs of the high sterns of their barques.

I hear the deep conch-shells, the martial horns
giving the rhythm to the flight of the oars;
the tumult is curbed by the clear song of the rowers,

and the Gods, on the heroic prow exalted,
with their antique smile and by the foam insulted,
reach toward me their indulgent sculptured arms.

CÉSAR

César, calme César, le pied sur toute chose,
Les poings durs dans la barbe, et l'œil sombre peuplé
D'aigles et des combats du couchant contemplé,
Ton cœur s'enfle, et se sent toute-puissante cause.

Le lac en vain palpite et lèche son lit rose;
En vain d'or précieux brille le jeune blé;
Tu durcis dans les nœuds de ton corps rassemblé
L'ordre, qui doit enfin fendre ta bouche close.

L'ample monde, au delà de l'immense horizon,
L'Empire attend l'éclair, le décret, le tison
Qui changeront le soir en furieuse aurore.

Heureux là-bas sur l'onde, et bercé du hasard,
Un pêcheur indolent qui flotte et chante, ignore
Quelle foudre s'amasse au centre de César.

CAESAR

Caesar, serene Caesar, your foot on all,
hard fists in your beard, and your gloomy eyes
pregnant with eagles and battles of foreseen fall,
your heart swells, feeling itself the omnipotent cause.

In vain the lake trembles, licking its rosy bed;
in vain gold glitters on the young wheat-straws;
you harden in the knots of your gathered body
the word that must finally rive your tight-clenched jaws.

The spacious world, beyond the immense horizon,
the Empire awaits the torch, the order, the lightning
that will turn the evening to a furious dawn.

Happily out on the water, and cradled in hazard,
a lazy fisherman is drifting and singing,
not knowing what thunder collects in the center of Caesar.

LA DORMEUSE

Quels secrets dans son cœur brûle ma jeune amie,
Ame par le doux masque aspirant une fleur?
De quels vains aliments sa naïve chaleur
Fait ce rayonnement d'une femme endormie?

Souffle, songes, silence, invincible accalmie,
Tu triomphes, ô paix plus puissante qu'un pleur,
Quand de ce plein sommeil l'onde grave et l'ampleur
Conspirent sur le sein d'une telle ennemie.

Dormeuse, amas doré d'ombres et d'abandons,
Ton repos redoutable est chargé de tels dons,
O biche avec langueur longue auprès d'une grappe,

Que malgré l'âme absente, occupée aux enfers,
Ta forme au ventre pur qu'un bras fluide drape,
Veille; ta forme veille, et mes yeux sont ouverts.

WOMAN ASLEEP

Within my young friend's heart what mysteries keep
aglow, soul from this sweet mask breathing a flower?
From what vain aliments does her candid ardor
kindle this radiance in a woman asleep?

Breath, silence, dreams, insuperable lull,
you triumph, O peace stronger than a tear,
when the heavy wave and vastness of this full
sleep in such an enemy's breast conspire.

Sleeper, golden heap of shade and surrender,
your formidable rest is laden with such boons,
doe among the grape-clusters stretched in languor,

that, though the soul be off in hell's communes,
your body with the pure belly a limp arm hides,
watches; your body watches, and my eyes are wide.

LE CANTIQUE DES COLONNES

Douces colonnes, aux
Chapeaux garnis de jour,
Ornés de vrais oiseaux
Qui marchent sur le tour,

Douces colonnes, ô
L'orchestre de fuseaux!
Chacune immole son
Silence à l'unisson.

—Que portez-vous si haut,
Égales radieuses?
—Au désir sans défaut
Nos grâces studieuses!

Nous chantons à la fois
Que nous portons les cieux!
O seule et sage voix
Qui chantes pour les yeux!

Vois quels hymnes candides!
Quelle sonorité
Nos éléments limpides
Tirent de la clarté!

Si froides et dorées
Nous fûmes de nos lits
Par le ciseau tirées
Pour devenir ces lys!

THE CANTICLE OF THE COLUMNS

Harmonious columns with
capitals day adorns,
embellished with real birds
that walk around the turns,

sweet columns, orchestra
of distaffs! Every one
sacrifices its silence
to be in unison.

—What do you bear so high,
equals in radiance?
—Desire of faultlessness
in our studied elegance!

We are singing all together
that we bear up the skies!
O solitary grave voice
who are singing for the eyes!

See what candid hymns!
What sonority
our limpid elements
draw from the clarity!

Out of our stone beds,
gilded and so chilly,
we were freed by the chisel
to become these lillies!

De nos lits de cristal
Nous fûmes éveillées,
Des griffes de métal
Nous ont appareillées.

Pour affronter la lune,
La lune et le soleil,
On nous polit chacune
Comme ongle de l'orteil!

Servantes sans genoux,
Sourires sans figures,
La belle devant nous
Se sent les jambes pures.

Pieusement pareilles,
Le nez sous le bandeau
Et nos riches oreilles
Sourdes au blanc fardeau,

Un temple sur les yeux
Noirs pour l'éternité,
Nous allons sans les dieux
A la divinité!

Nos antiques jeunesses,
Chair mate et belles ombres,
Sont fières des finesses
Qui naissent par les nombres!

Filles des nombres d'or,
Fortes des lois du ciel,
Sur nous tombe et s'endort
Un dieu couleur de miel.

We have been awakened
from our beds of crystal,
and we have been invested
by these bands of metal.

That we outbrave the moon,
the moon and the sun's glow,
everything's polished us
like the nail of the great toe!

Servants without knees,
smiles without a face,
the beauty before us is conscious
of the pure limbs' grace.

Reverently alike,
the nose below the molding,
and our precious ears are deaf
to the white weight we are holding.

A temple above the eyes
blind for eternity,
we go without the gods
toward divinity!

Our ancient youthfulness,
dulled flesh and lovely umbras
are proud of the artifice
born among these numbers!

Strong with the laws of the sky,
daughters of golden numbers,
a honey-colored god
falls upon us and slumbers.

Il dort content, le Jour,
Que chaque jour offrons
Sur la table d'amour
Étale sur nos fronts.

Incorruptibles sœurs,
Mi-brûlantes, mi-fraîches,
Nous prîmes pour danseurs
Brises et feuilles sèches,

Et les siècles par dix,
Et les peuples passés,
C'est un profond jadis,
Jadis jamais assez!

Sous nos mêmes amours
Plus lourdes que le monde
Nous traversons les jours
Comme une pierre l'onde!

Nous marchons dans le temps
Et nos corps éclatants
Ont des pas ineffables
Qui marquent dans les fables...

He sleeps serenely, the Day
whom we offer every day
upon the tablets of love
that our foreheads display.

Incorruptible sisters,
half-hot, half-cool, we've taken
for our dancers the breeze
and the leaves dry and shaken,

and the epochs by tens,
and bygone peoples untold
in a profound long-ago,
but never sufficiently old!

Heavier than the world,
bearing our own loves,
we journey across the days
as over a stone the waves.

We are walking into time
and our bodies shine
with steps ineffable
that are stamped in the fables . . .

NOTES

GÉRARD DE NERVAL (1808–1855), poet, romancer, and critic, deserves more attention than he usually gets. A translator of *Faust* (and praised by Goethe himself), he occupies a position in France as a champion of German literature similar to that of Coleridge and Carlyle in England. As a poet—a Romantic poet who almost saved himself—he adds a strange hermetic voice: often he seems to unify the aims of both classic and romantic literature in a technique that approaches that of the Symbolists. He certainly influenced Baudelaire and Mallarmé, and that is much for any man to have done. An amusing soul he was, too; he once took a live lobster for a walk beneath the colonnades of the Palais-Royal, on a leash of ribbon. But his frivolities turned to actual madness. In hospital, he placed on his own head the crown of flowers from a statue of the Virgin and paraded the aisles, laying his hands on other patients as one possessed of miraculous curative powers. At last, on a winter's morning, in a wretched alley, with some manuscript pages of his unfinished tale *Aurélia* in his pocket, he hanged himself with an apronstring which he imagined was the garter of a queen—an episode that later gave Mallarmé the concluding lines of "Le Guignon": "Ces héros excédés / De malaises badins / Vont ridiculement se pendre au réverbère" (These exaggerated heroes who have gone so far in drollery as to hang themselves on lampposts).

Vers dorés p. 2

This animistic poem first appeared in the periodical *L'Artiste* in 1845, a dozen years before Baudelaire's *Fleurs du Mal*, and its ninth line directs us to the opening stanza of the greater poet's "Correspondances," which attracted the Symbolists. The idea is also expressed in Gérard's never-finished *Aurélia*, chapter vi: ". . . everything in nature took on new aspects, and secret voices issued from plants, trees, animals, the humblest insects, to inform and encourage me . . . shapeless and lifeless objects offered themselves to the calculations of my mind;—I saw emerge from aggregations of pebbles, from contours of angles, cracks, openings, from denticulations of leaves, from colors, odors, and sounds, harmonies hitherto unknown. . . . Everything lives, everything acts, everything corresponds . . ." Baudelaire, who was not sympathetic to the cult of Nature, nevertheless voiced in

"Élévation" the pleasure of the poet "Qui plane sur la vie et comprend sans effort / Le langage des fleurs et des choses muettes" (Who, hovering over life, knows without trying / the tongues of silent things and of the flowers). Cf., for the opposite of the animistic doctrine, Housman's *Last Poems*, XL: "For nature, heartless, witless nature, / Will neither care nor know" what were a man's feelings and concerns. For "Vers dorés" Gérard borrowed the title, but nothing else, from the so-called "Golden Verses of Pythagoras," which had been translated into French. We may dismiss without comment the introductory Pythagore with his Gallic "Eh quoi!" The dictum, "Tout est sensible," repeated in line 8, could derive from any of seventy-seven ancients. Valéry liked the concluding line, in which, says Mlle Moulin, the alliterations in *r* and *s* "assist the desired impression of transparency and hardness." The poem reappeared in Gérard's *Petits Châteaux de Bohême*, 1853, which includes both prose and verse. In his later collected works it is one of the group called "Les Chimères," to which the next two poems also belong.

Delfica p. 4

The motto ("Now comes the last age of Cumaean song") is from Vergil's fourth Eclogue; the poem foretells a new golden age in poetry, and that prophecy was soon fulfilled. Daphne was a Thessalonian nymph who escaped the ardent Apollo by effecting, through prayer to a local river-god, an arboreal transformation that was to be immortalized later in pure Carrara marble by Canova: a girl caught in midflight and sprouting foliage everywhere. The Temple in line 5 is, I believe, that of Vesta at Tivoli (also called the Temple of the Sibyl); M. Maynial insists that it is the Temple of Isis at Pompeii, which the poet had visited with his fair traveling companion. Mallarmé was delighted to borrow—and without acknowledgment—line 6 for his poem "Le Guignon," line 9: "Mordant au citron d'or le idéal amer." Lines 7–8 were suggested by Goethe's "In Höhlen wohnt der Drachen alte Brut" (in Mignon's song, "Kennst du das Land . . ."). The grotto is the Sirens' Grotto, into which the waters of the Anio flow, and by implication that of the oracular Pythoness, priestess of Apollo at Delphi. Line 9 refers to the pagan gods allegedly vanquished by Christianity under the aegis of the Emperor Constantine, whose famous arch was erected shortly after 312 A.D.

Myrtho p. 6

Myrtho was apparently the same girl addressed as "Daphne" in the preceding sonnet, an English miss whom Gérard swam with, or thought he did, at Marseilles while awaiting passage by steamer to Italy (see the opening page of his *Octavie*). Posilipo lies on the coast at the foot of Vesuvius. In this memorable vicinity is produced the Lachryma Christi, a Neapolitan wine of comforting fortitude. Next to Liebfraumilch (the milk of the Virgin Mary) it is the most celebrated of wines of sacred origin. Line 7 is an elegant euphemism for being drunk on the floor. The astute Mallarmé has taken over lines 9–11 for his "L'Après-midi d'un Faune," near the finale:

> A l'heure où ce bois d'or et de cendres se teinte
> Une fête s'exalte en la feuillée éteinte:
> Etna! c'est parmi toi visité par Vénus
> Sur ta lave posant ses talons ingénus...

Line 12 refers to the capture of Naples in 1139 by Roger, King of the Two Sicilies, a descendant of the Norman duke Tancred. Vergil had a villa at Naples, and was buried, says Donatus, beside the highway to Puteoli; but his grave may now be under the waters of the Bay. Petrarch is said to have planted a laurel above Vergil's supposed tomb, thinking, rather inadvertently, of his own Laura. The Italians love such puns. M. Maynial maintains that the hortensia signifies modern times as compared with the myrtle of antiquity. This impossible grafting of the two different species was carefully copied by Baudelaire in "Les Deux bonnes Sœurs," line 14: "Sur ses myrtes infects enter tes noirs cyprès." What strange mélanges and sports we would have in our gardens if we took seriously the pseudo-dendrology of the poets—or rather, if nature did!

Fantaisie p. 8

Concerning this piece Gérard said: "En ce temps, je ronsardisais... " (At that time, I was Ronsardizing). He was also attracted to notions of reincarnation, and indulged a sort of dream life in which the Queen of Sheba would appear, or Marguerite de Valois, or Mme de Maintenon, or some other learned and lovely female—all of whom seem to have been mental forms of Jenny Colon, an actress with whom he had a hopeless love affair. His own name, Labrunie, seemed insufficient for such high company; he chose for himself the noble-sounding "de Nerval," and invented fittingly aristocratic genealogies. How perennial is the blonde in the tower! I believe she first appears —probably then a brunette—in one of the Egyptian stories translated by Maspero. Of course there is Jezebel, who looked down upon the mighty Jehu. There is Bluebeard's wife, who posted her sister Anne to survey the landscape for help. Every medieval castle seems to have had one; the list may conclude with the Lady of Shalott. In line 2, Rossini, Weber, and Mozart make a surprising trio: perhaps choice was influenced by metrical considerations, or perhaps Gérard wished

117

to compliment three musical nations—Italy, Germany, and Austria. In one version, he used the spelling "Wèbre," to match "funèbre." Read aloud, these sixteen lines produce thirty-five unforgettable French r's. I have managed some of them, but without the original resonance. The poem first appeared in the periodical *Les Annales romantiques,* in 1832. It influenced Baudelaire's "La Vie antérieure," which was printed in the *Revue des Deux Mondes* in 1855, after Gérard's death. In "A Une Passante," Baudelaire also celebrated the woman seen but once and never forgotten thereafter, who is the common property, though forever unattainable, of poets everywhere —in English, so familiar to us in "I did but see her passing by / And yet I love her till I die," set to music three and a half centuries ago. She is to be found in Verlaine's "Mon rêve familier" and, at a wry remove, in Corbière's "Bonne fortune et fortune."

CHARLES BAUDELAIRE (1821–1867) arranged his poems in a structural unity and presented them in a single volume, *Les Fleurs du Mal,* in 1857, the same year that saw the publication in book form of Flaubert's prose masterpiece, *Madame Bovary.* The government brought actions against both these writers as offenders against public morals. Flaubert was successfully defended. Baudelaire lost, and six of his poems were suppressed. But in preparing a statement for the lawyer who defended him, he had written: "The book must be judged as a whole; there will then be apparent its terrifying morality." And his contemporary, Barbey d'Aurevilly, who lived almost into our times, has said: "*Les Fleurs du Mal* was written in his blood and it is not only his personal history but that of the hypocritical reader, the modern man as he has emerged from the convulsions of the Revolution and of the nineteenth century." It is the most influential book of poems since Goethe. I have treated the *Fleurs du Mal* as a whole in my volume of translations from it (1947). Here, I must select a few poems that relate to the Symbolist movement—though Baudelaire preceded the Symbolists and founded no school himself, leaving, instead, a variety of spiritual heirs.

Élévation p. 10

An expression of the joy of the creative mind when it is exercising freely the power of thought. The sense of levitation is part of the Pegasus myth. M. Dondo points out that it is by the special function of the two final lines of the poem that "the frontiers between the feeling of the subjective and the objective have been broken down."

Correspondances p. 12

When Baudelaire uses nature as a setting, it is usually some exotic landscape, the background for a sensation or a woman. Here it seems to have a philosophical import; it is the phenomenon hiding the noumenon. (See Gérard de Nerval's "Vers dorés," above.) Perfumes and odors haunted him particularly, perhaps because of their very intangibility. Concerning his theory of *correspondances* he had already written in *Salon de 1846* on the symbolism of color, admitting his debt to Hoffmann, from whose *Kreisleriana* he cited the following: "It is not only in dreams, and in the light delirium which precedes sleep, but also on wakening, that I hear music, that I discover an intimate analogy between colors, sounds, and perfumes. The odor of red-brown marigolds produces above all a magic effect on me. It makes me fall into a profound reverie, and then I hear as if from afar the deep and solemn sounds of the oboe." In his analysis of the lyricism of Hugo, he wrote in *L'Art romantique*: "Swedenborg . . . has taught us that . . . everything, form, movement, number, color, perfume, in the spiritual as in the natural world, is significant, reciprocal, conversely related, and corresponding." M. Crépet has noted a source in Poe's "Al Aaraaf": "All nature speaks, and ev'n ideal things / Flap shadowy sounds from visionary wings." These ideas were doctrinal for the Symbolist poets.

Harmonie du soir   p. 14

Here, the perfumes, sounds, and colors of "Correspondances" *do* "correspond" in the Symbolist sense; they merge into one another— the perfumes and sounds into the movement of a waltz, the heart's agitation into the music of the violin, and the sunset sky into the image of an altar. The last line reveals the woman of whom the poet is thinking; and she has not merely been *in* the deserted garden, she *is* the garden. Her memory surrounds the poet. The perfumes of the flowers are hers; and those unexplained sounds, are they not her well-remembered voice? But that day is over, now; and the poet sees the darkness closing in as a black Nothingness. The violin will be heard again in Verlaine's "Chanson d'automne," and the enchanted garden will be reëntered in his "Après trois ans" and in Mallarmé's "Prose pour des Esseintes."

Spleen   p. 16

In four poems with this same title the poet is the personification of his own demon of Ennui. In its irritated state this ennui becomes what he meant by "spleen." And he has had much company in his unease; as Paul Desjardins was at pains to point out (*Revue Bleue*, 1887): "He exemplifies supremely a condition that modern man is conscious of . . . the distress of one who feels isolated and powerless, who is appalled by this and yet celebrates it . . . here is a private history that we know better than by hearsay." In the present

119

poem the metaphors of bureau, cemetery, boudoir, and desert are used to explore and outline an emotional state, an *état d'âme*, as the Symbolists called it. André Ferran writes of line 8: "The moon is a funerary star. The interior cemetery of Baudelaire is not even lighted by the moon." Nothing on a wall is sadder than a faded Boucher panel. The sphinx of the concluding lines is a memory of the "singing statue" of Memnon. Mallarmé will reset the granite block for his "Tombeau d'Edgar Poe."

Obsession p. 18

In *Les Fleurs du Mal* this poem follows the four on spleen, and its title confesses that the poet is completely under the dominance of his splenetic malaise. Advancing toward his finale, he attacks Nature in her grandest aspects—the forest, the sea, and the stars. M. Crépet quotes from Jean Pommier (*La Mystique de Baudelaire*, 1932) a diagnosis: the sonnet shows "the suffering of the poet who cannot look without reading or listen without hearing something said." And from Chateaubriand's *Génie de Christianisme*: "The groves were the first temples." Note that the "regards familiers" are now quite other than those of "Correspondances."

Le Soleil p. 20

In the 1857 edition of *Les Fleurs du Mal* this was the third poem in the book. Baudelaire must have thought highly of it, and it really does belong in that place because it deals (like the second poem, "Bénédiction") with the joys and powers of the poet. I enjoy the poet's telling how he dreams of his work as he walks around town. The use of metaphors is noteworthy; in fact, it has been the subject of at least one scholarly inquiry. The use of the word "vers" in lines 8, 10, and 11 is possibly a three-edged pun? The one in line 10 could mean 'worms'; the poet has discussed verses in his first stanza. He was, moreover, a vermiphile in excellent standing; worms are prominent characters in three of his poems, and are accessories in dozens of others.

PAUL VERLAINE (1844–1896), for a while a Parnassian, was too spontaneously tuneful, too mercurial in his moods, to remain long with any group of sternly sculptural and objective poets. He was full of music; and "musicalization" was a prime tenet of the Symbolists. Composers have set to music a large number of his poems, mainly as songs for voice and piano (though Stravinsky has written a score or two for full orchestra). It would be interesting to know if the musicians' tunes are in accord with what the poet heard in his head. The "Chanson d'automne" in his first collected volume, the *Poèmes saturniens* of 1866, is an unforgettable air on a melancholy flute. Its last stanza foretells his own future: he became the wind-blown leaf. (The story of his bohemian life of careless wandering and dissipation has been too often told to need repetition here.) But meanwhile there appeared other volumes from his hand: *Fêtes galantes*, 1869, delightfully artificial, like a series of colored engravings; *La Bonne Chanson*, 1870, personal poems, wistful and tender; *Romances sans paroles*, 1874, which contains much of his best work; and *Sagesse*, 1881, confessional lyrics written after his downfall. In *Jadis et naguère*, 1884, are collected a variety of pieces, some written in other periods; the most important of them is "Art poétique," adopted as a manifesto by the Symbolists. In his trio of slight prose sketches, the *Poètes maudits* of 1884, he beat the drum for Corbière, Rimbaud, and Mallarmé, and gave examples of their work.

Après trois ans　p. 22

At first glance this is a description of a garden revisited. But appearances are deceptive. The point is that *someone* is *not* there. And how different the bourgeois décor (M. Micha's apt phrase) from the castle-bower scenery of the romantics! Baudelaire had already made the shift, in his very short poem beginning "Je n'ai pas oublié... ," with its little white suburban house, its plaster Pomona and shabby Venus, and the late afternoon sun cascading "sur la nappe frugale et les rideaux de serge." Veleda, a Druid priestess and the heroine of an episode in Chateaubriand's *Les Martyrs*, was a popular subject for the ornamental statuary of French gardens in the early nineteenth century. In the last line, the somewhat affected "gracile" was used in translating "grêle" because the English and the French word have a common Latin origin.

Croquis parisien　p. 24

Here, almost for the first time, Verlaine speaks in his own voice; his earlier poems are more or less derivative. The far-fetched similes, the totally un-Baudelairean cat, and the paradoxical whimsy of Grecian dreams beneath Parisian gaslights constitute a signature beyond forgery. All the words of the second stanza bear the impress of his minting. The poem is one of the "Eaux-fortes" (Etchings) in *Poèmes saturniens*.

Chanson d'automne　p. 26

No one has ever translated, or can or will translate, this poem properly; yet it offers the supreme challenge, the shining lure of the bright impossible. Though it is words on the page, it is much more music that exists off the page. It is heard, and hardly seen at all.

Clair de lune   p. 28

This poem, from *Fêtes galantes,* is perhaps Verlaine's first purely Symbolist achievement. Notice that the lady's soul is the real subject; but the trope makes the poem. It is doubtful that he had any particular woman in mind. The mood was probably stimulated by some gay courtesan from the canvases of the painters about Versailles. The force of "choisi" is that it implies a landscape *composed* ideally by an artist, like Watteau.

Il pleure dans mon cœur...   p. 30

In line 1 the use of the impersonal verb, purposely vague, suggests that Verlaine connected the rain and the weeping with something external to himself: it is raining, it is weeping. Compare Tristan Corbière's "Le Poète contumace," sixth line from the end: "Il pleut dans mon foyer, il pleut dans mon cœur feu." The pun in line 10 is awkward in English. The indefinable grief seems more pathetic than the spleen of Baudelaire. This is one of the poet's masterpieces. It is from the *Romances sans paroles,* and has been set to music by Debussy.

Langueur   p. 32

This is a reminder that the Symbolist poets were first called Decadents, in part derisively, in part because they seemed afflicted with the *mal du fin de siècle*—a condition supposedly symptomatic of a declining, corrupt and vitiated, civilization. To be sure, these poets grew up in the aftermath of France's Second Empire; but Remy de Gourmont, as he looked back at the late 1880's and 1890's, the period of Symbolism's amplest flowering, objected: "*Décadence:* what a mistake! . . . Talents were born every day. As in the first stage of the world, there was a perpetual creation"—the reason for which he thought, should be looked for in "that development of individualism which accompanied the first years of the Third Republic. It was political liberty, boundless then, that engendered the taste for literary liberty. . . . The latest young writers . . . support the government (which is their affair); we others, fifteen years ago, we didn't even know there *was* a government. We enjoyed freedom to write, freedom to live, all the freedoms, and thought of nothing but expressing what was in our minds, even if it was a little mad." It is a common-sense view, perhaps a salutary offset to those philosophical *arrière-pensées* by which later critics explain poets as spokesmen of man's decline and fall. (At that rate, we should all have gone through the bottom long ago. Have we? It is always a debatable question.) Bathyllus, in line 10, was one of the pretty lads in the "Anacreontic" poems.

Art poétique   p. 34

Appearing first in the periodical *Paris-moderne* in 1882, this poem took its permanent place in *Jadis et naguère*, 1884, and supplied a quotable *ars poetica* for the Symbolists, who were already indebted to Poe's critical theories (by no means was his influence in France dependent on his weak verses) and to the influence of Wagner's music. Verlaine himself never lived up to the whole theory, for he loved rhymes too well. A French scholar—who insists on remaining anonymous—finally gave me the clue to the last stanza. One must imagine poetry, like a vagabond gypsy girl, running gaily along at dawn, singing carelessly, with "unpremeditated art." The final word of the poem is used, of course, pejoratively.

TRISTAN CORBIÈRE (1845–1875), a victim of tuberculosis before he was quite thirty, left one book of poems, *Les Amours jaunes*, 1873. It is astonishing stuff. And the poet is hardly to be classified; his place is like that of the man who won a seat in the French parliament by running as "an independent Independent." One meets him quite amiably in "Le Poète contumace." But it is his "Rondels pour après" that most clearly entitle him to inclusion here. (His variety— his poems of Paris, of the sea and sailors, of himself and his native Brittany—I have dealt with more fully in my volume of translations from his work.) The "Rondels" are, as M. Le Goffic has remarked, "a light-and-shadow poetry, rather whispered than sung, yet so musical, rich in faraway resonances and mysterious extensions, expression of a mood, unknown to the Parnassian generation, which was to become that of the generation of 1884"—that is, of the Symbolists proper. They have been set to music by Jean d'Udine (in the Paris music weekly, *Le Ménestrel*, 1923). There is a supermundane sweetness about them that has been equaled in lyrical poetry only by some of the songs of Shakespeare and the early poems of Blake. Even the almost meaningless evocations which begin several of them: "enfant, voleur d'étincelles" (child, thief of sparks), "méchant ferreur de cigales" (naughty blacksmith of the cicadas), and "léger peigneur de comètes" (nimble comber of comets)—even these fumblings in the abracadabra of poetry, these almost charlatan attempts to get a *spirituel* rabbit from a matter-of-fact prose hat, are powerful assertions of the legerdemain of the man. Yet there is a gravity about them, for they are hallowed by the radiant majesty of death.

Le Poète contumace   p. 38

Had Childe Harold, Childe Roland, or any other leading man of romantic poetry, ever happened on such a stage setting, he would have moved right in and felt at home. From romantic drama, one character's voice is actually heard: "Belles nuits pour l'orgie à la tour" pluralizes the opening remark of Orsini the innkeeper as the curtain rises on Act I, scene ii, of Dumas's *Tour de Nesle:* "What a perfect night for an orgy at the tower! The sky is black, rain is falling, the city sleeps, the river is rising as if to meet corpses . . . A wonderful night for love: outside, the roar of thunder; within, the clink of glasses, and kisses, and lovers' murmurings . . ." Corbière mentions the Tour de Nesle by name in another poem, "Gente Dame," not included in these translations. In the present poem, the very next line unexpectedly echoes Lamartine, whom the poet has earlier spoken of contemptuously. Corbière: "Nuits à la Roméo!— Jamais il ne fait jour." Lamartine (in the poem "Novissima verba"): ". . . notre cœur enchanté / Dit comme Roméo: 'Non, ce n'est pas l'aurore! / Aimons toujours: l'oiseau ne chante pas encore!' " But Tristan's bird, like the nightingale in Boccaccio's story, would have been singing all night long. At any rate, here the wandering poet settles, hunting a place to die, with his spaniel Tristan II, and Ennui (that faithful Achates of Baudelaire and Mallarmé), the ghost of a lost love, and a covey of careless owls; not to mention his jocular notion of a lease—a notion prompted by the two stanzas of "Le Grand Testament" (lines 990–998) in which Villon "transfers" to Jean Cornu the "garden" (prison, that is) "Que maître Pierre Bobignon / M'arenta, en faisant refaire / L'huis et redresser le pignon." Corbière had an ironic genius—there is no other word for it—which saved all this. He writes down the hermit poet's story in an imaginary letter to the lost one; then he tears it up (after carefully preserving copies) and gives it to the winds. It is no pale Epipsychidion who inhabits this tower. Corbière's humor, and the very irony with which his self-pity is tempered, produce a fine poem. Right at the start, in the first introductory stanza, he engages our interest and amuses us. A deserted convent—hmm! But then *voilà!* come those darling donkeys, nibbling away at the shabby ivy on the tower wall, or the turret has a roof like a peaked hat knocked down over one ear! How well he understands these Bretons!—the gossips, the mayor, and the curé all come briefly alive. The hurdy-gurdy and the spaniel, the fields of golden broom, the Armorican heather, the periwinkle dying on a wall, the old poacher who comes at night to sit by the fire—all these sudden pictures make the thing vivid and viable. Corbière has been reading Bernardin de Saint-Pierre and Defoe, he remembers all the right people.

Castagnoles may be the fish called pomfrets (*Brama raii*), which skip vigorously when stranded on a beach; or wooden billets of the kind used to tighten awning-ropes on a vessel. Inès de la Sierra requires some documentation. Her story is from Gautier's poem "Inès de las Sierras" in *Émaux et camées* (1852), which derives from Charles Nodier's romantic novel *Inès de Las Sierras* (1837). Three French officers in Spain come to an old, deserted house: "un vrai château d'Anne Radcliffe" (with some bats by Goya). While they are at supper a vision appears: a woman dancing in black-and-white ribbons; her robe is dank from the tomb and straw-flecked; a faded yellow rose sheds its petals in her black hair, and a fine great wound makes a vermilion gash on her breast. That's enough to show why Inès was used in the poem at hand. Piously Corbière adds a trio of saints: Hubert, Anthony, and Thomas. "Sister Anne," watching from the tower for signs of approaching help, is from Perrault's telling of the Bluebeard story. The "chaumière" in the penultimate stanza is from Bernardin de Saint-Pierre's *La Chaumière indienne*, most likely; at any rate, from one of the Back to Nature idyls so dear to French sentimental romanticism. Although the poet complains of bad weather, he is doing all right when he can pick a batch of mushrooms on his cellar stairs, have plenty of broom for fragrance and color, and a fire of heather, briar, and driftwood. But he is really sad, as the sixth line from the end confesses—the line paralleled by Verlaine in "Il pleure dans mon cœur / Comme il pleut sur la ville."

The image of the pieces of torn letter vanishing in the fog is an ideal conclusion. But Tristan's subscribed note, as if he had written the poem at Penmarc'h, at Christmas time, must be looked into. After poking around this district two days, futilely, looking for such a place, I conclude that Tristan imagined even the tower. Nor could I find any such cliffs. M. Le Dantec, whose notes and critical introductions to *Les Amours jaunes* I recommend to all readers, says that the poem was written at Morlaix on the Christmas of 1871.

Rondel   p. 50

Addressed to himself—for he knew he was going to die—this little poem has a magic, indefinable, light as thistledown, evanescent as a bubble. Lines 2 and 3 are indebted to a passage in Bridaine's famous sermon on Eternity: "Eh! savez-vous ce que c'est que l'éternité? c'est une pendule dont le balancier dit et redit sans cesse ces deux mots seulement dans le silence des tombeaux: Toujours, jamais! Jamais, toujours!..." (see the chapter on Bridaine in Cardinal Maury's *Essai sur l'éloquence*), which also prompted Longfellow to write—how differently!—"The Old Clock on the Stairs." The bears that throw paving stones are borrowed from the one in La Fontaine (the tenth fable in book VIII) which crushed a fly on the friendly old amateur gardener's nose by smashing it—and the man too—with a "pavé."

But it is the music that matters, Verlaine's "la musique avant toute chose." Sing it, memorize it, love it, and you will have some of the secret of Corbière's charm. All these rondels are self-valedictory wavings of the hand: he is giving himself a going-away party. His hand is at his lips, bidding adieu.

Do, l'enfant, do... p. 50

This one follows logically enough. The Italian salutations move progressively from early evening to the final good-night. My line 5 will remind anyone of "Fear no more the heat o' the sun. . . ." *Fesse-cahier* is a term of denigration applied to any mere drudge of the pen, a bank clerk, lawyer's copyist, or, as Corbière means here, a hack reviewer. Cf. Goethe's "Proktophantasmist" in "Walpurgis Nacht," *Faust* I. The French call gossamer "the thread of the Virgin," which is doubly charming when one considers that our English word came from "goose summer," the season when geese were eaten and cobwebs drifted about.

Mirliton p. 52

The eternal shrill tintinnabulation to be heard in summer wherever cicadas tenant the fields is caused by vibrating membranes on the underside of the insect's abdomen. The blacksmith mentioned by the poet might imply someone who helped file the scraper or beat out the plates with which the almost metallic noise is made. One must avoid the notion that the winged creature needs shoeing, like a horse. The *muguet* is the flower that all France uses for May Day, when every marketplace is literally white with the bouquets and people delight in giving them, even to strangers. With a dozen such weapons a tourist can have himself quite a time with the pretty girls along the streets and at the sidewalk cafés. And all lovers feel it a cultural obligation to go off in the neighboring woods to gather their own flowers. This must all be understood to explain the irony the use of the flower has here. In the penultimate line, "les pâles," the bloodless ones, are of course the dead; the poet whose songs once could pierce the marrow of the living must now, being dead himself, sing for his pale countrymen.

Petit mort pour rire p. 52

Here we have a plaintive and faraway piping, frail as the soughings of the *mirliton* (reed-pipe) itself. These are songs without words, *chansons sans paroles,* as much as anything ever written. They are elegiac zephyrs blowing over a grave on which grows the *myosotis,* the forget-me-not. And they are the very devil to attempt in rhyme, for here one needs five or six rhymes on one sound. A

Petrarchan octave asks only four! These rondels are what M. Arnoux considers "a naked cry, the twisted heart, the words torn from their natural meaning, in a frenzy which evades both language and grammar." There is something in that line, "Va vite, léger peigneur de comètes," which haunts me, and it is by this phrase—the comet-comber—that I always think of Tristan.

Stéphane Mallarmé (1842–1898), a French teacher of English to French students, was a minute investigator of words, and contrived a kind of poetry that used words and combinations of them at the farthest possible remove from the expected. Thibaudet, one of his best critics, says that "his ideal would be to write the characters (like Chinese ideographs) in juxtaposition with neither phrase nor grammatical logic; no order of syntax would deform the purity of the words . . ." In the face of that I can only say: Listen again to Debussy's "Prelude to the Afternoon of a Faun," for Debussy will long remain as one of the best guides into the mysterious realm of Mallarmé, and it is finally as pure music that his poetry is best apprehended and enjoyed; as for understanding, that is another matter. Remy de Gourmont has said it better: "Mallarmé is the best pretext for reveries." In the struggle between the frozen lack of communication on the printed page and the fascination offered by an occasional glimpse into something rich and strange, the reader is battered about like a shuttlecock. But just when he is most annoyed, bored with these unsolvable riddles, maybe an indelible phrase will strike him and, like Saul on the road to Damascus, he will be ever afterward a changed man. Even Mallarmé's peers and col-leagues—Yeats, Rilke, Heredia, Valéry, D'Annunzio, Stefan George, Verhaeren, Coppée, Villiers de l'Isle Adam, Verlaine, to name a few—who attended reverently the famous Tuesday evenings in the cramped apartment on the rue de Rome, were never able to record the marvelous monologues he uttered while rolling and smoking in-numerable cigarettes. And there were, hélas, no tape recorders. But he did say: "La Pénultième... est morte," which might have been his own epitaph, for with the death of perhaps his most faithful dis-ciple Valéry, Symbolism, as a literary movement, may be said to have ended. His "Après-midi d'un Faune" first appeared in 1876 and, revised, in 1887; his Poésies, in 1887 and 1899.

Salut p. 54

On a first reading, this curtain-raiser of Mallarmé's Poésies will mean little to the uninitiated reader. The occasion for which it was written may somewhat apologize for and clarify the obviously in-tended feeling of obfuscation he wanted to give. As toastmaster for

127

a banquet by the review *La Plume,* in 1893, Mallarmé, the acknowledged *maître* of the younger writers, rises to his feet and clears his throat, in which death already had announced its intentions by making the voice sound husky. Delicately, almost diffidently, this little gray man lifts a glass of champagne in one hand and deftly produces—with somewhat of a magician's air as he fetches forth the rabbit from the silk hat—the manuscript of the sonnet that had finally satisfied him, after Lord knows how many hours of refining and condensing. His method was always that of the silversmith who arranges elaborately yards of fine wire, solders them into an inch-small butterfly, and says, "Voilà!" The effort is no longer apparent: the work of art remains, a unified, organic thing. He immediately admits that it is "Nothing," and thereby disarms potential opponents. The virgin verse and the foam on the wine are of equal value, delightful and evanescent. In the half-light of the banquet room the pale liquid in the glass may well have seemed almost invisible. Only a few bubbles indicate ephemerally the limits of the container. The play of gleams and shadows makes him think of supernatural aqueous creatures, suddenly reduced in size, and he pretends to see a group of sirens bathing and diving; nor could his Gallic mind resist the temptation of pointing out the pulchritude of these callipygic young women. (This preoccupation with the nude is characteristic of much of his verse.) Now, on this ocean conjured by his imagination, as captain of the vessel embarked on the perilous voyage of a literary life, he speaks from the poop to the young sailors, his disciples, who *are,* he says, the prow of his ship and are narrowly aware of the chill thunder crashing around the bold cutwater. Admitting himself to be a bit high, he humorously protests that he can stand upright holding his glass, like the tulip that suggested to Hafiz the figure of the steadfast tippler. With no fear of the pitching deck—i.e., the floor which may already have seemed to be revolving gently—he names "Solitude, star, rock-coast," all of which are the sailor's background and destiny, and proposes his toast to whatever it may be that is worth the chiseling and polishing, the night-vigils and soul-sweat, the loneliness and lack of appreciation that go into the making of poetry, "the white concern of our sail." It is also characteristic that he willfully switches the adjective. Nor does he speciously promise a safe harbor after the voyage.

L'Après-midi d'un Faune   p. 56

The "Faune" is as shy as a young deer, and only several readings will gain its confidence—unless it be that Debussy will also help, for he has understood the intention better than the critics do. The highest pleasure one can get from it will be from the musical quality of the words themselves, in their seemingly careless but so artful and willful disarrangement from syntax and their intolerance of the common decent rules of coherence. Presumably, the Faun symbolizes man's dream-desires; at any rate, he is alive and vigorous as the little satyr playing with the nanny-goat in *il cabineto segreto* at the Museum of Naples, devoted to the erotica discovered in the ruins of Pompeii and Herculaneum. In the scene's lush setting, near a swamp, primitive desire is wide awake. The Faun feels that he must possess one of the bathing nymphs. Failing that, he picks up a couple of them, sleeping in each other's perilous arms. When they too escape him, he contents himself with blowing bubbles from grapeskins, a symbol of intoxication. Or at least, this is how it all seems to him. He falls asleep—and the reader shares his dreams. This poem has had more influence and has received wider circulation than any other in the *Poésies*. Bakst presented a ballet production, under the direction of Diaghileff, with Debussy's music, and Nijinsky danced as the Faun! It should have been good, and apparently it was. Praised by Rodin, but attacked by *Le Figaro*. Perhaps the most important influence of the "Faune" was on Valéry's two Narcissus poems and *La Jeune Parque*. It also offers as good an opportunity as any to demonstrate the difference between Symbolist and other French poetry of the time. As the late Albert Schinz discovered (see *Modern Language Notes*, November, 1937), Mallarmé was thoughtfully acquainted with Leconte de Lisle's "Pan" (in *Poèmes antiques*, 1852); he included it in a selection of French poems appended to *Les Dieux antiques* (1880), a French adaptation of Cox's Mythology which he did for the publisher Rothschild. Discussion is not necessary; one has only to compare the two poems. "Pan" is fortunately only twenty-four lines long, and so can be included here:

PAN

Pan d'Arcadie, aux pieds de chèvre, au front armé
De deux cornes, bruyant, et des pasteurs aimé,
Emplis les verts roseaux d'une amoureuse haleine.
Dès que l'aube a doré la montagne et la plaine,
Vagabond, il se plaît aux jeux, aux chœurs dansants
Des Nymphes, sur la mousse et las gazons naissants.
La peau du lynx revêt son dos; sa tête est ceinte
De l'agreste safran, de la molle hyacinthe;
Et d'un rire sonore il éveille les bois,
Les Nymphes aux pieds nus accourent à sa voix,
Et légères, auprès des fontaines limpides,
Elles entourent Pan de leurs rondes rapides.

129

Dans les grottes de pampre, au creux des antres frais
Le long des cours d'eau vive échappés des forêts,
Sous le dôme touffu des épaisses yeuses,
Le Dieu fuit de midi les ardeurs radieuses;
Il s'endort; et les bois, respectant son sommeil,
Gardent le divin Pan des flèches du Soleil,
Mais sitôt que la Nuit, calme et ceinte d'étoiles,
Déploie aux cieux muets les longs plis de ses voiles,
Pan, d'amour enflammé, dans les bois familiers
Poursuit le vierge errante à l'ombre des halliers,
La saisit au passage; et, transporté de joie,
Aux clartés de la lune, il emporte sa proie.

Sainte p. 64

A beautiful little poem, almost pious, as lucent as a sunlit window in Chartres Cathedral. It is written in one sentence, divided by a colon so that the result is a diptych. St. Cecilia would seem to be the subject of the first part. Whether she is concealing be a *viole* or a lute is not the point, because she is not playing it, but points to an old hymnbook, doubtless of vellum, with magnificent rubric and probably square notes in the score. Notice how a faraway-and-long-ago feeling is given by such words as "santal," "vieux," "jadis," "mandore." In the second part the action is sharply concentrated on "balance," and the piece ends with an eternal suspension: an unplayed chord on an unplayable instrument. The saint here is shown against a monstrance window, i.e., a very glittering bit of glazing, though the monstrance proper would be an "ostensoir," a gilded vessel faced with a sunburst and containing the Host. Mallarmé employs the term to give a feeling of religious dignity and splendor to his poem. She seems to be playing on the spread wing of an angel who is going home at evening. This looks like a large harp, so she playfully "balances" her delicate fingers above the wing and the rest is silence. Truly, "Heard melodies are sweet, but those unheard / Are sweeter." Once—and he stresses the word by using it twice,—once there was music of the Magnificat, a fine hymn, supported with viol, mandore (an instrument like a mandolin), and flute. But a new music, a music of silence, is now suggested. The rhymes are of two sorts: those with full, open sounds, like *dédore, mandore, ostensoir, soir,* and the muted nasals, *recélant, étincelant, étalant, ruisselant, Ange, phalange, balance, silence.* It is an effective device for producing unity. "Sainte" is one of the most delicately conceived of all Mallarmé's production. By way of contrast, one may notice the beginning of "Vitrail," by Heredia, which opens: "Cette verrière a vu dames et hauts barons / Étincelants d'azur, d'or, de flamme et de nacre . . ." Thereafter a fine stained-glass window is expected, but the whole poem is concerned with the ladies and nobles, their petty occupations, and their stone effigies on tombs. It is a fine sonnet, but something very different, with its sonorous words, rich metals, and glittering colors, its mention of falcons and crusades. It is a Parnassian piece, a rather chilly, calm statement. There is nothing haunting or evasive about it, as there is about "Sainte."

Prose   p. 66

The fastidious hero of Huysmans's *A Rebours*, with his somewhat affected artificiality and ultrasensitivity, admittedly owes something to Mallarmé. Thus the present poem becomes almost a soliloquy in which the duke, or poet, remembers a mental experience so vividly that it often seems to be actually taking place in the present tense. The title implies "a hymn or rhythm introduced into the Mass . . ." I have chosen to rhyme only the second and fourth lines because an octosyllabic quatrain in English loses the dignity necessary to sustain the grave, liturgical tone demanded by the title. Since in much of the poet's best work the intention has been to produce incantation rather than exposition, suggestion rather than statement, the piece should be read aloud several times to get the effect of this quality. One hears the stiff metallic rhythm, the hidden alliterations that lull the reason, and the trisyllabic rhymes work on the reader with the drowsy repetitive beat of voodoo drums heard in the jungle of the subconscious. Notice the following: *spirituels–rituels, de visions–devisions, se para–sépara, désir Idées–des iridées, monotone ment–étonnement, par chemins–parchemins,* and *aïeul–glaïeul.*

Visual images emerge no less clearly. One may come more easily to comprehend the dramatic values if he imagines a dim figure, the precentor who intones the poem, before a Gothic lectern on which a solemn incunabulum with leaves of parchment the color of old ivory, provided with a heavy wrought-iron clasp, is spread open. (Such a volume, containing a magic ritual for the initiates of poetry, must be kept locked, against profane eyes. Notice, too, that while in "Sainte" such a volume is open on the Magnificat, a similar effect of mystery is here achieved.) It begins with an almost cabalistic word, "Hyperbole!"—extravagant exaggeration of statement, the essence of this highly artificial Byzantine type of poetry. The present hieratic volume seems to be a compendium of the knowledge of the Middle Ages, almost as if it had been compiled by an Albertus Magnus. We are being inducted into a hymn that is "spirituel" rather than "spiritual," and he thus limits narrowly an understanding audience, and purposely. One reads in all of Mallarmé's critics that this is a

131

charming memory of a brother-sister experience from his childhood. Stuff, sentimentality, and nonsense! Not at all! The following stanzas lead one into a poetic interpretation of a subconscious experience undergone by a strange twin-sibling from some unknown mythology, something akin to the first hermaphroditic creatures imagined by Aristophanes, according to Plato, or the Chinese *yin* and *yang* in the circle, or even those mythical Chinese birds (*pi-i*) that have only one wing and must hence fly ever joined together. This double-mind, almost in a trance, has given itself to remembering an almost lost earlier vision in which the feminine part is seen as more closely related to Nature than the observing masculine side. (Remember how one always feels this relationship of flowers, swelling fruit, and tree limbs to woman's charms.) But the visionary, the poet and artist, is always in conflict with the upholders of "authority": the pundits, critics, and little academicians. Such folk can see nothing in this ideal island, this garden of the lost Atlantis or Utopia, a sister-country to Möricke's "far-gleaming Orplid." Stanza 6 means that here the true seer beholds the ideal-reality, while the visionary (in a pejorative use of the word) perceives only his visions that are no more than the products of the imagination. There is no need of talking, for the twin-halves communicate silently. These flowers have the reality of the noumenon and may be said to be products of "the artifice of eternity" (Yeats), the same flowers that one finds in Mallarmé's "Toast funèbre":

> . . . pourpre ivre et grand calice clair,
> Que, pluie et diamant, le regard diaphane
> Resté là sur ces fleurs dont nulle ne se fane,
> Isole parmi l'heure et le rayon du jour!

And further, these flowers are from "the true groves" of poetry.

After "long desire" the poet understands these noumenal flora and is stimulated to a new consecration: his duty to receive and create for the lower world what he has experienced. So he goes back to work, "his ancient care," while the intuition merely needs smile and do nothing about it. And here is partly explained the difficulty of the last two stanzas. The feminine has forever existed in the state of Being as "Pulcheria" (archetypal Beauty), while the masculine must strive, in a state of Becoming, to achieve it. Yet, by its very nature, art (the "too great irises") obscures as with a veil the ideal. This is much the same stuff as those final lines in *Faust* II: "Das Ewig-weibliche / Zieht uns hinan." In the fairy story it is the child who sees the giant beanstalk, and the poet as seer pierces farther than the power of mere reason into this country in that magic ocean in which "full-fathoms-five"-drowned kings drift in blue querns of chalcedony; this country seen through "magic casements, opening on the foam / Of perilous seas, in faery lands forlorn." It lies somewhere beyond Yeats's "dolphin-torn, that gong-tormented sea."

The poet—who is forever young—pries beyond what is available to the concepts of the platitudinous world with its everlasting repetitive susurrus monotonously drumming on his "juvenile surprise" that such a place cannot exist.

I have nowhere found for the last two stanzas any explanation that I can accept. The apparent dichotomy of the twin-being that now receives two names seems deliberately stated. The name "Anastase" (Anastasius) has been made important in the Eastern Empire by a patriarch of Antioch, two emperors, and three popes. It certainly bears relation to ἀνάστασις, 'resurrection.' But the feminine twin has "resigned her ecstasy" and uttered the cabalistic name as "born for eternity." This is the end of the unmarked quotation, and I refuse to believe that she is buried at all—for is she not immortal as a Platonic idea: an archetype, a being beyond time and death? What the phrase "her ancestors" means is beyond me, but *his* name must imply the poetry written under the spirit of what is called Byzantine, and this can best be defined by a poet who also practiced, in a later time, the same sort of art. Yeats was for a while a disciple of Mallarmé and sat at his feet during some of the famous Tuesday evenings on the rue de Rome. From his two poems on the theory of such creation is a strange stanza partly defining it; the work of an ideal poet is one of those "monuments of unaging intellect," of

> . . . such a form as Grecian goldsmiths make
> Of hammered gold and gold enamelling
> To keep a drowsy Emperor awake;
> Or set upon a golden bough to sing
> To lords and ladies of Byzantium
> Of what is past, or passing, or to come.

It is certainly not clear who is buried or what is the antecedent of son aïeul." I am sure that she says only "Anastasius, born for parchments of eternity," though the poet does not punctuate it so. If he is entombed, so much the worse, but her mockery implies that *even* if he were to be buried, her name (strangely in a Latin form) could not be seen because the too great (exaggerated) flower of his work and imagination would obscure the ideal never to be attained by any artist. This is related to a line in "Les Fenêtres": "A renaître . . . / Au ciel antérieur où fleurit la Beauté" (To be reborn . . . / in the anterior sky where Beauty flowers). I take it that "anterior" means the ever-existing Nowhere, the very "sol des cent iris," the ideal rooting place of Beauty where the two parts of one spirit were still together: the relation of Becoming to Being. (Even Botticelli could not paint the idea of Beauty, but we remember her beautiful handmaid, the sea-born Venus on the great shell as she draws near to shore: Beauty seen in a tangible art-form.)

Autre éventail   p. 70

Mallarmé's genius is concealed precisely in his manner of dealing with seemingly trivial things so that they are endowed with an import far greater than their face value. This is perhaps best seen in the short-line last sonnets; but here is an example already at hand, which may justifiably excuse omission of those poems. "Autre éventail" is for the poet's daughter Geneviève, who was then twenty, a fairly pretty blonde whom Whistler painted in gray and rose—and a charming thing he made of it! The father used to write playful verses on Easter eggs, in red and gold ink; now his grateful love for her leads him to place a scepter in her hand and leave her, graciously poised in eternity. Debussy set the poem to music in 1913. What a threefold bid for artistic immortality the girl has! The fan is whispering to her on a warm summer evening: she is ripe for romance but as yet untouched by it. Any French girl of Mallarmé's social class is usually well protected by a vigilant mother. The play of the fan-strokes creates a microcosm in the slight segment of a circle comprised by its movements. But the poem thrusts forth the radial ribs of the fan until they grow so far apart that only the horizon can put an arc to it. This is the true power of poetry. Now all space trembles, like the great kiss formed invisibly on the girl's wistful mouth. But there is no objective for the impulse, so it is turned off into a smile that slips from the corner of her lips into the "unanimous crease," the compact folds of the fan. Then the girl poses its rose and gold, like a little queen's scepter, so that it contrasts with the ruby or garnet bracelet. Very pretty; a perfect bijou of playfulness.

Le Tombeau de Charles Baudelaire   p. 72

Baudelaire died in 1867. The greatest poet of France must have a monument, and at once! So, in 1892, La Plume, which seems to have been particularly astute and prompt about such matters, appointed a committee: Mallarmé, Heredia, Leconte de Lisle, Verlaine, Verhaeren, Huysmans, Stefan George, and others—a committee of genius if ever there was one. With the celerity characteristic of such bodies, plans were made and briskly pushed, and nine years later the monument was finished—thirty-four years late. The tomb itself is some distance away from the site of the monument. Mallarmé was describing some plan, real or imaginary; it is possible that he had seen one. And the poem is misnamed. The monument presents a figure swathed in wrappings like a mummy but with the head bare, stretched on a slab a few inches above the ground; a stele rises behind, and at the top of this the upper half of a figure that reminds one of "The Thinker" gazes gloomily at the effigy; and a bat or lizardlike creature is crawling up the stele. It is really quite monstrous in its effect. I prefer to pay homage to the unassuming tomb, where other members of the family are also buried, one above another. Occasionally, at Toussaint, I have found a small bunch of flowers or so, and have several times left one myself; but I prefer to sit there and read some of the poems. Mallarmé describes an imaginary monument, to his liking. It interests me that he could have been in the graveyard by lamplight, for the cemeteries are always closed at six o'clock in summer and at five in winter. And how could he have seen that gas lamp? Or maybe the walls are a recent erection. Anyhow, Anubis, the jackal-headed Egyptian god that leads the soul off to judgment, is appropriate enough, for Baudelaire liked to write about wolves. Mallarmé gets his muck and rubies from Baudelaire's "Le Vin des Chiffoniers":

> Souvent, à la clarté rouge d'un réverbère
> Dont le vent bat la flamme et tourmente le verre,
> Au cœur d'un vieux faubourg, labyrinthe fangeux
> Où l'humanité grouille en ferments orageux...

Mallarmé probably saw the sunken grave before the tomb was installed. No, it's older than that. They certainly can't shove a ton of stone aside, to open a grave. I'm at a loss about what he saw. All critics agree that the lamp with the besotted twisted wick represents the attacks made on *Les Fleurs du Mal*, the "opprobres subis" by the government and some of the reviewers. "Cities without evening" would be cemeteries, of course. But the dead poet needs no wreaths of homage, because his Shade seems to brood there. The poison is the effect of the *Fleurs du Mal*, and it is "tutelary" because the complete effect of the book is a deadly morality.

Mes bouquins...   p. 74

Poets are always very careful about choosing the first and last poem of a volume. Why was this one chosen for a finale? Here sits Mallarmé, his feet on an andiron shaped like a mythological wyvern, something like a cockatrice. He is surrounded by his books. Outside, the wind is blowing loose snow sharply across the ground. Everything about the poem deals with something finished, dead, negative, nonexistent, fabulous, or in some way or other unreal. His books are

135

old, they are *closed*, and on the name of a *dead* city. He chooses a *ruin*, past its triumphant days. Let the *cold* scythe-like wind blow the snow off and reveal the naked earth, it has spoiled everything for him by making the landscape *too real*. His hunger that will feast on *no* fruits here finds in their *absence* an *indifferent* taste, although one of them, probably his wife, warm human flesh, bursts with yearning for a bit of attention. Feet on a *wyvern* where love stirs the fire, he broods longer *desperately*, on the *ancient Amazon's seared* breast. He is satisfied with nothing present, real, or human, but wants the far-away, the defunct, the unreal landscape. He wants some absent fruit, the nonexistent Amazon's lost breast. For she had sacrificed it, you remember, to increase her skill as a toxophilite. Mallarmé once wrote to Carondel: "Mon art est une impasse." He is right, but Valéry sits at the end of the cul-de-sac, as the final disciple of a sterile art. *He* will not leave any heirs. If the end of this blind corridor could be opened, there would be only *Le Néant, le gouffre* of Baudelaire.

ARTHUR RIMBAUD (1854–1891), the *enfant terrible* of this poetic period, wrote all his poems in his teens. From his home town near the Belgian border he went to Paris in 1871 and met Verlaine, who soon left wife and child to wander with the young man in Belgium and England. Their *Wanderjahr* ended when Verlaine shot him (with so wobbly an aim that Rimbaud was not much hurt). Verlaine went to prison. And Rimbaud parted company with poetry. In 1875 he entered on a life of adventure: drifted about Europe, enlisted in the Dutch army and deserted in Java, made his way back to France and went to Egypt and Cyprus, and spent eleven years on the Somali coast and in Abyssinia as the agent of a French exporter. He tried unsuccessfully to make quick money by gun-running, with Menelek for a customer. Disease drove him home, and in search of improved health he died in a hospital in Marseilles. As a poet, he was like those men of violence who, as St. Matthew tells, take the kingdom of heaven by force. He was impatient and undisciplined, and wrote with a violence at times brutal, often with the set purpose of shocking his readers. His more legitimate efforts have an acid bite, an ironic impact, that is peculiarly his own. It is a precocious poetry, welcomed by his Symbolist contemporaries for the vigor of its imagery. Some of his work appeared scatteringly in magazines, and some was not published until after his death. His *Poésies complètes* were first issued, with a preface by Verlaine, in 1895.

Le Dormeur du val p. 76

This poem, which first appeared in the publisher Lemerre's *Anthologie des poètes français*, 1888, is dated October, 1870. The

Franco-Prussian War had begun, and it is possible that Rimbaud saw some incidents; his native town, Charleville, was in the war zone. The young soldier asleep here is very dead: direct notation (with compassion) has replaced vague rhetoric (with *la gloire*); perhaps the only parallel is O'Connor's general in the Civil War piece, ". . . face turned to the sky, / And beaten by the rain." The whole ironic intention of the poem is left till the last line—and that is the way sonnets should be written. Observe, for contrast, the melancholy failure of many of Shakespeare's final couplets.

Les Chercheuses de poux   p. 78

A minor masterpiece, with Baudelairean blending of the senses. The reader is alternately pleased, disgusted, fascinated, and sympathetic, all in twenty lines. The setting is an orphans' home. The "sisters" are nuns, for had they been the boy's own sisters, one at a time would have done the job. The origins of the Gothic were from the same cold misty land, the Ardennes, where Rimbaud was born, and naturally he uses the mixture of the ugly and the beautiful. The utter wistfulness of the child in the last stanza is quite touching—perhaps the poet's most humane lines.

Le Bateau ivre   p. 80

The boat speaks, communicating a series of visions like the broken episodes of a dream. Rimbaud has completely rewritten and upset Baudelaire's "Le Voyage" in a manner both amusing and exciting. The experiences herein were purely imaginary and indebted to various travel books, but what a triumph of make-believe! And when the virgin lava of this young man's steamy brains erupted, not a little havoc was occasioned on the calm and laureled slopes of Parnassus. Here is a new cacophonic music of sometimes incoherent ejaculations, with strikingly accurate seascapes that are more remarkable than those of Coleridge, who also had not seen the ocean. Henri Béraud, in his article "Sources d'inspiration du Bateau ivre," in the *Mercure de France* (1922), mentions Gautier as an indubitable influence. But there remain also Hugo's *Travailleurs de la mer* and Jules Verne's *Vingt mille lieues sous les mers* to be considered, and of course the boy had read them both. Poe's *Narrative of Arthur Gordon Pym* and *Descent into the Maelstrom,* available to him in Baudelaire's translations, must have given him suggestions. Leconte de Lisle and Heredia, with their oceans and forests, their panthers and serpents, and their profoundly moving plastic images, certainly influenced the young poet. But even this Parnassian material he has recast in anti-plastic musicalization that makes his poem one of the cornerstones of Symbolism.

Stanza 1: "Haleurs" are towers; at first, the boat was guided with ropes by men moving along the riverbanks. But the Redskins (out of our own Fenimore Cooper) disposed of them.

2: Rimbaud already fancied himself as an importer; later he was a trader's agent in Abyssinia.

3: The world's peninsulas are likened to boats, as if they could cast off from the continents. In fact, everything is transmuted and given the power of navigation.

4: The "falots" are lanterns on shore, for warning or guidance; they mean security, but the boat prefers the storm.

5: Valéry will use the simile of the fruit-eater, in the third stanza of "Le Cimetière marin": "Comme le fruit se fend en jouissance... "

6: The ocean itself becomes a poem, and images of sea and sky are merged; the stars in the deeps of the heavens are in the ocean deeps too.

7: The English adjective "rutilant," which means 'glowing with a ruddy or golden light,' has a history from the fifteenth century to George Moore, and I have not hesitated to adopt Rimbaud's "rutilance" as the corresponding noun.

9: The "figements" in line 2 were perhaps suggested by Baudelaire's "Harmonie du soir," line 12: "Le soleil s'est noyé dans son sang qui se fige." The reference to the actors, line 3, may be related to them: the blinding of Oedipus is a bloody spectacle—as also is the blinding of Gloucester in *King Lear*. In line 4, the waves' "frissons de volets" are related to the flicker that occurs when the leaves of an interior window-shutter are made to turn, or to the pattern of parallels which then appears on the floor, sunlight being admitted from without.

10: Phosphorescence is perhaps the most beautiful of all night phenomena at sea. By transference from sight to sound, the poet makes it sing.

11: Medieval legends credit the Virgin with power to calm the waves, and there is a Provençal version in which three of the Marys of Biblical times miraculously got safe ashore. Again Rimbaud mingles two startling images: the waves charge at the rock ledges like maddened cattle; and the bright feet of the holy women, walking the water, press muzzles upon them, checking their bawling.

12: The "incroyables Florides" are scenes that French readers of travel books had from print and quite naturally thought improbable—perhaps something like the jungle pictures of the painter Rousseau: big leaves, snakes, et cetera.

15: The "dorade" is our dorado, or dolphin, which has golden sides. It is a sea creature notoriously fond of music; cf. the Arion story. To say that it actually sings is stretching the point; but it does have a mild grunting bark, at least during the mating season, for I have heard them in the Caribbean Sea.

17: "Presqu'île" in some editions; Verlaine corrected it to "presque île" in his copy. Well, a ship is hardly a peninsula, but it is very like an island that moves.

18: The Monitors in line 3 are not Ericsson's invention, but French war vessels of a kind known to Rimbaud's day, armored three-deckers with sails and auxiliary steam power. The vessels of the Hanseatic League must have resembled those of Columbus.

19: It was dirty weather, with snotty cloud-wraiths shot with sun-patches.

21: Fifty marine leagues, which reckons out at 172.5 miles, is a long way to hear a whirlpool, much less the roaring of a lecherous hippopotamus. Rimbaud here mixed suavely the Bible and Poe.

22: "Vogueur" in line 2 is an archaic word, to be found in Littré if not in modern dictionaries.

25: I have seen "pontons" translated as "scows" and "barges," neither of which will do. "Hulks" was the common English name for the kind of floating prisons used in English ports at the time of the Napoleonic Wars (see, e.g., *Vanity Fair*, chap. xxxi) and later for convicts (as in the opening chapter of *Great Expectations*).

The poem first appeared in the periodical *Lutèce*, in 1883. It had been written a dozen years earlier; when Rimbaud arrived in Paris in September, 1871, he had it in his luggage. Isn't it a fine sea-poem from a boy of seventeen who had never been to sea? I am not aware that Melville or Conrad, experienced tars, did any better in their prose.

JULES LAFORGUE (1860–1887), born in Montevideo, was educated in France, and was lucky enough to hold for five years the position of court reader to the Empress Augusta in Berlin. His work has been acknowledged as one of the most stimulating sources of inspiration for modern poetry, equally with that of Corbière and Rimbaud. But of the capricious, original, and bizarre quality of these poets, most of the divine afflatus seems to have evaporated between the cup and the lip. Laforgue and his young wife died of tuberculosis and the German winters, in the same year. And so many fine second-rate poets have lived to be octogenarians! Laforgue, Rimbaud, and Corbière are certainly the trio most interesting after the greater Baudelaire, Verlaine, and Mallarmé. Of the perverse three, Laforgue was the foremost proponent of logodaedaly, tripotage, and steganography, and in his chosen field he was the complete virtuoso. More than any other poet here represented, he demands an equally cold

139

ironic interpretation from his translator—*that* has afforded no little difficulty; and his linguistic audacities have given me more trouble than the work of any other poet. He should have done them in English himself. His *Les Complaintes* appeared in 1885; *L'Imitation de Notre-Dame la Lune*, in 1886; other poems were gathered, after his death, in *Les Derniers Vers*.

Complainte des pianos p. 88

The poet goes for a quiet walk ("chaste flânerie": not a woman-hunt) at early evening, without his topcoat, and the eternal ice-chopped-in-a-sink of those Chopin études, from the open windows of girls' boarding schools, further distresses his shattered nerves. He imagines the claustral life of the inmates, with Jesus and the janitor as the only available males on the premises. He imagines their adolescent dreams and frustrations. His rhythms change with his verse patterns: a quatrain, a couplet in long meter, a short couplet, a final choppy quatrain, then the whole is repeated again and again, like the ritornelle itself. It is maddening. The short quatrains in quotation marks are the thoughts of the girls, and their theme is always that of the languid possessive feminine after the eternally elusive male. His double-entendres must not be underrated; for instance, "la bonne blessure," and the brisk masculinity of "un train-train pavoisé d'estime et de chiffons." "Le pure flacon... baptisé" is the same thing as the "vase profond" in Baudelaire's "Le Beau Navire." At the end of the poem appears the street-name "Rue Madame." Whatever the rue Madame may have been in Laforgue's day, it is different now; but maybe he was merely malicious in calling this section of Paris a "better neighborhood."

Complainte de l'oubli des Morts p. 92

This writer is both precocious and *précieux*, a literary dandy who a century before, would have been a *muscadin*. How the old dowagers of the court must have shuddered at—and just loved—his shocking verses! But this bright young man is dying of a febrile disease, dying, yet he still mocks at death, like some heroic gamin of the Revolution, shot in a gutter. The vocabulary is difficult, the rhythm and meter constantly varied, so that the reader finds himself dancing to an orchestra that plays snatches of waltzes, two-steps, rhumbas, and polkas. Yet much of Laforgue's work, that seems to have been carelessly tossed off, is so intellectually chiseled to precision and emotionally controlled that the result is a *chatoyance* rivaled by no other French poet and found only in Mercutio at the hour of his extremity.

Dimanches p. 96

Little girls from French *pensionnats* are always to be seen on the Parisian sidewalks, like the children in Blake's "Holy Thursday": "It was on Holy Thursday, / Their innocent faces clean, / Came children, walking two by two, / In red and blue and green." Only —the French children usually wear a dark nondescript uniform. The little suicide at first reading might seem to have been depressed because she lacked the nicer clothes of her comrades. But remember the subtitling quotation. Well, the girl is dead, and *nil nisi bonum*... Had there been a handy Newfoundland around, she would have been saved.

Albums p. 98

How accurately the poet, who had never visited America, has caught the spirit of California! Only the note about tattooing is far-fetched. It took a prophet to announce, more than sixty years ago, the development of religious cults, especially south of the Tehachapi.

Notre petite compagne p. 100

Here, Laforgue seems to be telling us that the woman always wins, but that even she does not know why—though she knows very well how to go about it. It is always man's judgment on woman, that she is no philosopher and (is she right, after all?) doesn't need to concern herself with reasons; while man, who unfortunately thinks about it, is thus doubly defeated in his naïve attempt to be partners with the Eternal Feminine. Originally included in the projected *Fleurs de bonne volonté*, which Laforgue dropped in 1886, this poem was used almost verbatim in *Le Concile féerique*, his dialogue poem in which a Lady and a Gentleman exchange their views on the eternal theme of Woman.

PAUL VALÉRY (1871–1945), disciple of Mallarmé, had an early success as a poet in the 1890's, and then went into a long silence, busying himself with mathematics and philosophy, until in 1917, with the publication of *La Jeune Parque*, he found himself like a sculptor who had chiseled a great statue without a pedestal. In 1920 there appeared *Le Cimitière marin* and *Album des Vers anciens* (a collection of his earlier work); in 1921, *Le Serpent*; and in 1922, *Charmes*. His collected *Poésies* were published in 1942. Most of his shorter poems are in the nature of supporting décor for his *chef-d'œuvre*, but the sonnets have a life of their own. As the last Symbolist, and perhaps the most confirmed proponent of the dicta of the movement (with a rather too arrogant and highfalutin notion of himself as arch-poet for me to stomach readily), Valéry in his work may be said

141

to deal more with the genesis and the making of poetry than with creating what I might call "easel pieces" that can stand on their own claims. Mallarmé had dreamed of "a book that would be a book, architectural and premeditated, and not a collection of chance inspirations however marvelous in themselves." Certainly all Valéry's work shows that he is essentially a man of thought rather than of feeling, but I have long been annoyed by his "refusal to describe" attitude. Either a poet has powerful ideas and emotions that must, like murder, out, or he hasn't. I have left for the Notes (below) a splendid example of a poem about the making of a poem that illustrates what is to be expected of this cerebral type of thing. But certainly the Helen and Caesar sonnets need no such explanation. Each is a symbol, of course, of a supreme beauty or a supreme man of power. And each is a clearly apprehensible picture that the reader is at no loss to see instantly. So much for his "refusal to describe."

Hélène p. 102

Helen of Troy revisits a royal waterside, and her hands remember the beards of long-departed kings. The change of tense emphasizes the abyss that only memory can bridge. Past and present merge. Merely by announcing herself, she fills her present—and our present, too. And her memories summon up the past, both sights and sounds, with marvelous vividness.

César p. 104

Vast as Michelangelo's "Meditative Knight," and with even greater implications, this figure is not only Caesar but Mussolini, though the poem was written long before the Fascist assumption of power. Epic material is concentrated into slight space, horizons are prophetically overridden, and history tags along to bear out the portent within such a man. That happy little fisherman is typical of the dumb Remi, or Remuses, who are necessary by millions to support one Romulus.

La Dormeuse p. 106

All French nudes, in verse or painting, have a tendency toward sleek bawdiness. This poem has more delicacy and catches some of the breathless quality, almost awe, that one might feel on discovering a sleeping nymph. She might have come from Giorgione's "Sleeping Venus," for the pose is the same. I should have liked to have left this simple and charming picture without further comment, to have stolen away, like a gentleman. But no! the critics and professors, as gauche and crude as newspaper gossipmongers, must rush in, awaken the girl and ply her with questions about how it feels to sleep under a vine and what was her visit in hell like. The half dozen books and articles on my desk, from Thibaudet to Walzer, a Professor Grubbs, and several lady writers—I could collect a welter of fluttering dithers stirred by these good people as they solemnly write about treatments of subjects, analyses, origins, psychological approaches, specific content, etc. The poetic afflatus is supposed to be awakening a dream in the weary girl, until she is possessed by inspiration, as by a god. One goes so far as to contend that the young girl is a future sonnet and not a girl at all! Moi, I'll take the girl any day.

Le Cantique des colonnes   p. 108

This constitutes part of the peristyle erected for *La Jeune Parque,* almost like Bernini's colonnades before St. Peter's. I like to think he got the inspiration from those beautiful, lonely columns remaining from the Temple of Hercules at Agrigentum. They are finer than any in the Roman Forum. If it was somewhere in Athens, I have missed them. And really what an unusual conception behind this poem! But rarely has the "frozen music" which is architecture melted into such a lyrical and ethereal art-form. It's pretty hard to imagine Notre-Dame bursting into a Bach mass, and only the windows in Chartres, on a sunny day, really sing. But here the group of columns is like a chorus of Grecian girls, so very feminine and graceful, like distaffs because such pillars are almost perceivably larger in the middle than at the ends (to give the illusion that they are straight rather than, so to speak, "sway-backed"). They are as reverent as grave priestesses, yet womanly enough to know their beauty, and playful enough to love the dancing leaves that swirl about their feet. They have beheld the march of generations of people, of many centuries, yet suddenly they stand as of the present, and firmly stanced to march on into time, bearing the profound language of other aeons and the evidence of the abiding mathematics of the disciples of Plato, Pythagoras, and Euclid who built them so surely, so masterfully.

Valéry's Narcissus poems are too long for translation here. And the famous *Cimetière marin* has been translated several times. As a finale, I would rather justify the statement of the critic Thibaudet, who sounded the mort-note of such poetry when he wrote: "Valéry forced poetry to leave the sentimental and pass to the metaphysical." But despite the high achievements of the English school of that name —a misnomer, at that—metaphysics and poetry are not bedmates.

Here is a poem in which the poetry lies in discussing the making of poetry—we have come that far from the real thing, charming as his essay, disguised in beautiful verse, may be. Valéry brings into

143

"Aurore" three *deae ex machinà,* Confidence, Prudence, and Hope.
May I be allowed to break the continuity by a running *explication?*

AURORE

The morose disturbance
that served me in sleep's despite
vanishes at the appearance
of the sun's rose light.
In my soul I advance,
all winged with confidence:
the day's first orison!
Scarcely clear of the sand,
boldly I make some grand
steps in the hall of reason.

The poet wakens after a bad night, rubs "sand" from his eyes and,
inspired by Confidence, begins to write. He gathers his tools of
verse-making.

Friendly similes, hail!
Sparkling under the thin
words—from slumber still pale,
you with the smiles that are twins!
Basketfuls I will gather
among the bees' loud pother,
and my prudence giddy
on the trembling rung has put
firmly her candid foot
on the gilded ladder already.

He goes into the garden of his imagination and meets Simile and
Rhyme—the twins. But Prudence, a charming nymph particularly
French (at least, up to 1918), is already taking over, with critical
pruning-shears. The bees represent classical restraint.

What a dawn on these hilltops
that are beginning to quiver!
They stretch themselves, these groups
that seemed to be sleeping forever;
one yawns and one shines,
a lazy one entwines
in her shell comb a choice
dream that near by lingers,
waylaying it with vague fingers
as the premises of her voice.

144

From the misty hills of semiconsciousness advance the Ideas, pleasant young nymphs, sleepy, but not stupid and languid as are the odalisques of Ingres. These are real as Degas's dancers who hitch up their tights and scratch their backsides. They are now addressed by the poet as if they were those harlots of Lautrec.

> What! is it you, rumpled trulls?
> What were you up to last night,
> Ideas, mistresses of my soul,
> courtesans out of spite?
> —And they answer, always clever:
> Our immortal presences never
> yet have betrayed your roof!
> Secretly all night through
> we span our webs, not aloof,
> within the darkness of you!

More like an indulgent father than a jealous lover, the poet playfully upbraids them for their dishabille. But they know all the answers: We didn't leave the house for a single minute! All night we were working away at the web of your Freudian dreams. So much for these very modern young wenches! They continue:

> Will you not be drunken once
> of joy? From the dark to see issue
> a hundred thousand silk suns
> on your enigmatic tissue?
> See, what we've done is this:
> over your abyss
> we have stretched our primitive
> threads and have taken bare
> Nature in a spare
> loom of preparatives.

You old stodgy! they are teasing him. Can't you ever let yourself go and feel the Dionysiac joy of creation when we've done overtime among your dream associations—when you were blacked out in your abyss"—to get something ready for you this morning? But the stern classicist refuses such accidental felicities:

> I break their spiritual
> web and go to hunt
> in my forest sensual
> the oracle of my chant.

145

> Being! Cosmic ear!
> All my soul with desire
> wholly unites . . . and trembling
> gives herself to her dream
> and sometimes my lips seem
> to catch her shuddering.

He will have no dream-caprices. When he writes, he wants to be awake in the forest of his alert senses. His soul—and that implies with Valéry the stimulations of his thyroid and adrenal glands—is in accord with his wish to create. So reason goes forth to harvest his rich domain.

> Here my vines are shady,
> the cradles of my chances!
> The images are so many
> they are equal to my glances . . .
> each leaf tendering
> to me an obliging spring
> whence I drink this frail bruit . . .
> each kernel, all pulp implicit,
> every calyx solicits
> that I await its fruit.

Every experience may contain his good luck. ("Nothing is ever lost," said Rilke.) He has refused the offerings of the subconsciousness and seeks only from real experience. In the following stanza we find the thorns symbolizing the difficulty of composition as an act of volition

> I do not fear the spines!
> The warning is good though severe!
> These ideal rapines
> do not want anyone to be sure:
> to ravish a world is no wound
> so sharp, so profound,
> that would not to the ravisher
> be a wound, fecund and rich,
> to assure his own blood which
> is the real possessor.

These difficulties, the spines, obstacles to be overcome, afford the creator a masochistic joy through pain involved in struggle. "There is a pleasure in poetic pains," said Wordsworth. It was such labor kept Dante lean, drove Verlaine to absinthe, and Nerval to suicide

But Valéry, already with a calm eye on the Academy, goes cautiously
ahead, lured by his third goddess, Hope.

> I approach the limpid brimming
> of the invisible glade,
> the pool where my Hope is swimming,
> her breast borne up by the flood.
> Her neck cuts the misty air
> and raises this wave which prepares
> her a matchless collar. She
> feels that beneath the wave flows
> boundless profundity,
> and she shudders from her toes.

Here Valéry errs gravely by changing metaphors. He has been
picking fruit throughout, now this bathing-beauty takes over, swim-
ming so fast that she wears a collar of foam. Foam and fiddlesticks.
Hope should have come in with a fine basket of fruit. Instead, she
takes a dip! But her shudder is the true *awe* of poetic struggle with
the deep unknown. That is valid enough; but no goddess should have
cold feet.

In this poem about the making of a poem, we come to the final cap-
sheaf of a slender harvest of Symbolistic verse. It is as bad as "the
meaning of meaning of meaning," yet Valéry is the last great poet
of France, that is to say, of Europe and America. Baudelaire has had
his revenge. All his sons are dead. And Pegasus has lifted his great
wings and flown off to some less bloody planet. We have discovered
the imponderable *nouveau* of "Le Voyage," and the news has been
bad.

Mallarmé concluded his sonnet "Le vierge, le vivace et le bel
aujourd'hui" with

> Il s'immobilise au songe froid de mépris
> Que vêt parmi l'exil inutile le Cygne

"swathed in futile exile with a chill / dream of contumely, the Swan
is still." Valéry is the dead Swan.

BIBLIOGRAPHY

[This brief bibliography is necessarily selective, since a great deal has been written about Symbolist poetry, much of it in critical studies of poets discussed separately. Included below are general works which I have found helpful, and details identifying certain books and articles which are referred to in the Notes by author's name only. —C.F.M.]

Ajalbert, Jean. *Mémoires en vrac. Au temps du Symbolisme, 1880–1890.* Paris: Michel, 1938.

Arnoux, Alexandre. *Une âme et pas de violon: Tristan Corbière.* Paris: Grasset, 1930.

Arréat, Lucien. *Nos poètes et la pensée de leur temps.* Paris: Alcan, 1920.

Barbey d'Aurevilly, Jules. Letter in appendix to Baudelaire's *Fleurs du Mal,* edition of 1868.

Barre, André. *Le Symbolisme.* Paris: Jouve, 1911.

Bowra, C. M. *The Heritage of Symbolism.* London: Macmillan, 1943.

Brunetière, Ferdinand. *L'Évolution de la poésie lyrique en France au XIX* siècle.* 2 vols. Paris: Hachette, 1894.

———— *Histoire et littérature.* Paris: Calmann-Lévy, 1884.

———— "Symbolistes et Decadens," *Revue des Deux Mondes,* 1** novembre 1888.

Carrère, Jean. *Les Mauvais Maîtres.* Paris: Plon-Nourrit, 1922.

Charpentier, John. *Le Symbolisme.* Paris: Les Arts et le Livre, 1927.

Clouard, Henri. *Histoire de la littérature française du Symbolisme à nos jours.* Vol. I: *1885–1914.* Paris: Michel, 1947.

———— *La Poésie française moderne.* Paris: Gauthier-Villars, 1924.

Crépet, Jacques. Notes to the edition of Baudelaire's *Fleurs du Mal* by Crépet and Blin. Paris: Corti, 1942.

Dondo, Mathurin. "Baudelaire et la poésie incantatoire," *French Review,* March-April, 1936.

Dujardin, Édouard. "La Vivante Continuité du Symbolisme," *Mercure de France,* 1** juillet 1924.

Ferran, André. Notes to *Poésies choisis* of Baudelaire. Paris: Hachette, 1937.

Fiser, Éméric. *Le Symbole littéraire.* Paris: Corti, 1941.

Fontainas, André. *Mes souvenirs du Symbolisme.* Paris: Nouvelle Revue Critique, 1928.

France, Anatole. *La Vie littéraire*. 3d series. Paris: Calmann-Lévy, 1891.

George, Stefan. *Zeitgenössiche Dichter*. Berlin: Bondi, 1905.

Gosse, Edmund. *French Profiles*. New edition. London: Heinemann, 1913.

Gourmont, Remy de. *Le Livre de masques*. 2 vols. Paris: Mercure de France, 1896 and 1898.

────── *Promenades littéraires*. Paris: Mercure de France, 1904.

Gregh, Fernand. *Portrait de la poésie moderne de Rimbaud à Valéry*. Paris: Delagrave, 1939.

Houssaye, Arsène. *Les Confessions*, Vol. I. Paris: Dentu, 1885.

Huysmans, J.-K. *A Rebours*. Paris: Charpentier, 1884.

Kahn, Gustave. *Les Origines de Symbolisme*. Paris: Messein, 1936.

────── *Symbolistes et Décadents*. Paris: Vanier, 1902.

Lalou, René. *Histoire de la littérature française contemporaine*. Paris: Crès, 1922. English translation by W. A. Bradley, *Contemporary French Literature*. New York: Knopf, 1924.

Le Dantec, Yves-Gérard. Critical notes to editions of Baudelaire, Verlaine, and Corbière; especially to two editions of *Les Amours jaunes*—Paris: Émile-Paul frères, 1942, and Gallimard, 1953.

Le Goffic, Charles. Preface to his edition of Corbière's *Amours jaunes*. Paris: Messein, 1926.

Lemaître, Jules. *Les Contemporains*. Four series. Paris: Lecène et Oudin, 1885–1889.

MacIntyre, C. F., trans. [Baudelaire:] *One Hundred Poems from Les Fleurs du Mal*. Univ. of California Press, 1947.

────── [Corbière:] *Selections from Les Amours jaunes*. Univ. of California Press, 1954.

────── [Mallarmé:] *Selected Poems*. Univ. of California Press, 1957.

────── [Verlaine:] *Selected Poems*. Univ. of California Press, 1948.

Martino, Pierre. *Parnasse et Symbolisme*. 9th edition. Paris: Colin, 1954.

Maynial, Édouard. *Anthologie des poètes du XIXᵉ siècle*. Paris: Hachette, 1935.

Mazel, Henri. *Aux beaux temps du Symbolisme*. Paris: Mercure de France, 1943.

Micha, Alexandre. *Verlaine et les poètes symbolistes*. Paris: Larousse, 1943.

Michaud, Guy. *La Doctrine symboliste*. Paris: Nizet, 1947.

────── *Message poétique du Symbolisme*. 3 vols. Paris: Nizet, 1947–1948.

Moréas, Jean. "Les Décadents," *Le XIXᵉ Siècle*, 11 août 1885.

────── Manifesto for Symbolism, in supplement to *Le Figaro*, 18 septembre 1886.

Moulin, Jeannine. Notes to her edition of Gérard de Nerval's *Les Chimères*. Lille: Giard, 1949.

Poizat, Alfred. *Le Symbolisme de Baudelaire à Claudel*. Paris: Bloud et Gay, 1924.

Raymond, Marcel. *De Baudelaire au Surréalisme*. Paris: Corrêa, 1933. English translation: *From Baudelaire to Surrealism*. New York: Wittenborn, Schultz, 1949.

Raynaud, Ernest. *En marge de la mêlée symboliste*. Paris: Mercure de France, 1936.

—— *La Mêlée symboliste*. 3 vols. Paris: La Renaissance du Livre, 1918–1923.

Reynaud, Louis. *La Crise de notre littérature*. Paris: Hachette, 1929.

Romanic Review. "The Poetics of French Symbolism" [a symposium: papers on Baudelaire, Mallarmé, Rimbaud, Valéry], Vol. XLVI, No. 3, October, 1955.

Rudler, M. G. *Parnassiens, Symbolistes et Décadents*. Paris: Messein, 1938.

Schérer, Edmond. *Études sur la littérature contemporaine*. 10 vols. Paris: Calmann-Lévy, 1885–1895.

Symonds, Arthur. *The Symbolist Movement in Literature*. London: Heinemann, 1899.

Thibaudet, Albert. *La Poésie de Stéphane Mallarmé*. 3d ed. Paris: Nouvelle Revue Française, 1926.

Valéry, Paul. Preface to Lucien Fabre's *Connaissance de la Déesse*. Paris: Société littéraire de la France, 1920.

—— *Variété*. 3 vols. Paris: Gallimard, 1930–1936.

Van Bever, Ad., and Paul Léautaud. *Poètes d'aujourd'hui*. 2 vols. Paris: Mercure de France, 1900.

Verlaine, Paul. *Les Poètes maudits*. Paris: Vanier, 1884.

Vigié-Lecocq, E. *La Poésie contemporaine, 1884–1896*. Paris: Mercure de France, 1896.

Wilson, Edmund. *Axel's Castle*. New York: Scribners, 1931.